open-plan living

open-plan
living

CYNTHIA INIONS

photography by ANDREW WOOD

RYLAND
PETERS
& SMALL

LONDON   NEW YORK

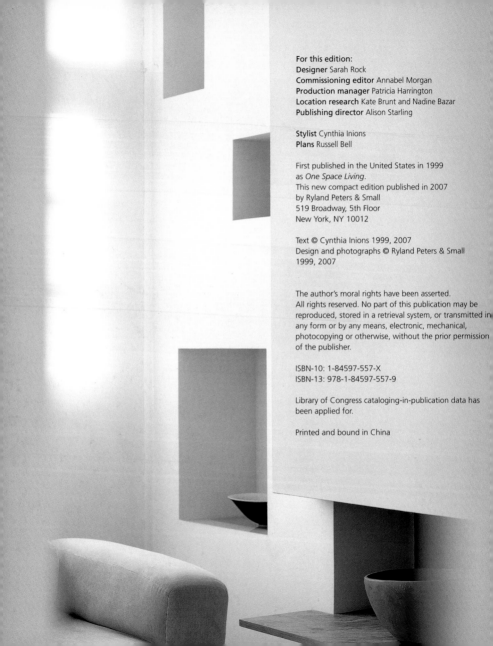

For this edition:
Designer Sarah Rock
Commissioning editor Annabel Morgan
Production manager Patricia Harrington
Location research Kate Brunt and Nadine Bazar
Publishing director Alison Starling

Stylist Cynthia Inions
Plans Russell Bell

First published in the United States in 1999
as *One Space Living*.
This new compact edition published in 2007
by Ryland Peters & Small
519 Broadway, 5th Floor
New York, NY 10012

ISBN-10: 1-84597-557-X
ISBN-13: 978-1-84597-557-9

Library of Congress cataloging-in-publication data has
been applied for.

Printed and bound in China

contents

introduction

For more and more people, an open-plan home is the solution to the challenge of contemporary living. Open-plan living offers the freedom to organize our homes to suit the new informality in the way we live and spend time with family and friends, the diversity of fast-paced modern lifestyles, and the demand for a multifunctional environment.

Designing and planning an open-plan living environment from scratch, or simply revising a conventional interior, presents an opportunity to use the available space more efficiently and imaginatively, to create a welcoming and flexible home environment, and enjoy a new sense of light, openness, and integration. Introducing permanent partitions or reconfiguring your space with flexible dividers can provide a comfortable degree of separation between public and private areas without compromising the overall unity or versatility of the space.

The open-plan home utilizes a new and dynamic vocabulary of space, light, and freedom of choice. This book presents an inspiring collection of many different open-plan environments, from radical conversions of former industrial buildings to simple low-level reworkings of typical domestic interiors, from cutting-edge concrete and glass constructions to family-friendly environments abundant with color and comfort.

opposite A dynamic conversion of a mail-sorting center provides a versatile split-level open-plan interior. **above left** Flip-up and pull-down panels can expose and enclose different elements of this kitchen area as desired. **above right** In a two-level loft, knocking through from one floor level to another to create a mezzanine level radically improved the light distribution and sense of openness.

open-plan
living

why open-plan? I options I help

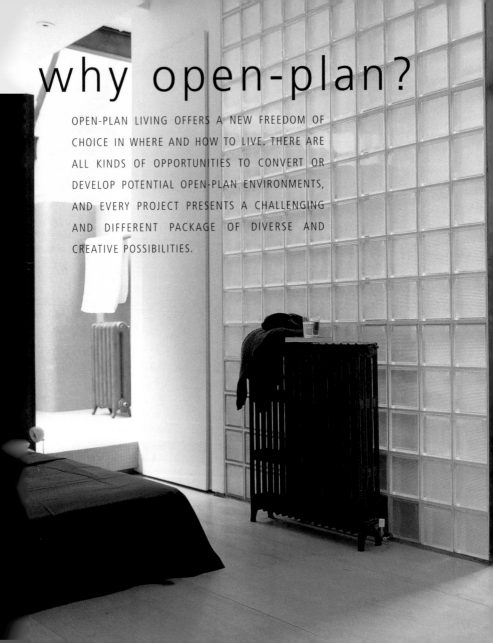

why open-plan?

OPEN-PLAN LIVING OFFERS A NEW FREEDOM OF
CHOICE IN WHERE AND HOW TO LIVE. THERE ARE
ALL KINDS OF OPPORTUNITIES TO CONVERT OR
DEVELOP POTENTIAL OPEN-PLAN ENVIRONMENTS,
AND EVERY PROJECT PRESENTS A CHALLENGING
AND DIFFERENT PACKAGE OF DIVERSE AND
CREATIVE POSSIBILITIES.

Freedom

In an open-plan environment, everything is up for review. Conventional ideas about designing and planning a domestic interior are irrelevant—in an open-plan home, there is no need to separate and confine everyday activities within a restrictive traditional layout. Whether you reconfigure a conventional space, take on an existing open-plan scheme and adapt it, or convert a previously non-domestic unit, the design and planning decisions will always be specific to every project.

Of all the possibilities, converting or refitting a non-domestic environment offers the maximum creative freedom. It allows you to develop an original space, removed from any references to domestic architectural proportions, structures, and materials. Alternatively, stripping a domestic interior to an empty shell and beginning again can be an equally exciting undertaking. Nevertheless, it's important to be aware that projects like these are expensive undertakings that require a great deal of commitment, time, and energy.

Less ambitious schemes offer varying degrees of creative freedom. Sometimes an existing interior can be modified and improved by opening up the space. Introducing uniform floor coverings or lighting systems throughout can bring a new sense of integration and harmony, and create the impression of spacious open-plan living without entailing massive disruption or expense.

left The raw architecture of a former printing factory provided an inspiring start for this new domestic space. Visible metal support beams, concrete paving-slab flooring, and heavy-duty professional catering equipment are in keeping with the industrial aesthetic of the space.

OPEN-PLAN LIVING OFFERS AN OPPORTUNITY TO MAKE THE MOST OF YOUR AVAILABLE SPACE

Sense of space

above left and opposite In a loft conversion, removing part of an upper floor and adding a double-height window optimizes light and space.
above center The mezzanine level provides a series of areas for relaxing, sleeping, bathing, and working. Sliding panels make flexible dividers.
above right The sleek, minimalist kitchen area is kept deliberately free of clutter, adding to the overall sense of space and light.

A sense of space is life-enhancing and makes all the difference between a dynamic, welcoming environment and an unappealing one. Open-plan living offers the opportunity to make the most of your space, whatever its size or shape.

There are many different ways to create or increase a sense of space, from large-impact structural alterations to a simple process of paring down and elimination. Radical transformations, like removing walls or floors to create a double-height space, increasing the size of windows, or converting redundant roof space, will all increase a feeling of openness and improve light distribution

However, maximum openness is not always the best way forward. In conventional interiors, it is not always possible to remove internal walls, either for structural reasons or because imposing a radical open-plan layout will spoil the overall proportions of the space. If this is the case, reducing the size of walls, either vertically or horizontally, adding portholes, or creating internal windows will all provide a degree of openness and sense of connection while preserving original divisions and supports.

Reorganization on a smaller scale can also help to increase the perception of space. Getting rid of excess furniture and clutter is an effective and immediate way to increase space. For example, keep only "enough" chairs around a table, and store any extras. Keep kitchen surfaces clear and stack magazines and books in storage systems. Everything, no matter how appealing or valuable, takes up space, so subtract anything unnecessary or excessive and see the difference.

opposite In an industrial conversion, lightweight paper screens are used to define and separate different areas. The screens can move to suit changing needs.

left and below Precise planning and high spec details, like this folding, curving screen, provide maximum flexibility in a tiny townhouse conversion.

Flexibility

Open-plan living has potential for maximum flexibility, allowing you to optimize space. The traditional Japanese interior demonstrates how to manipulate space to suit different activities by using panels or screens to sub-divide a single unit into different configurations. This principle of dividing a space to provide degrees of separation and privacy without compromising a sense of unity is a good model for contemporary environments.

Paper blinds, freestanding screens, and fabric dividers all work effectively as low-cost, temporary fixtures. For example, a bathroom in an open-plan bedroom gains privacy when screened with a length of fabric, while an apartment can be sub-divided into separate living and work areas by ceiling-to-floor lengths of paper hanging from hooks. Architectural devices such as transparent or solid panels, rotating sections of wall, and doors that fold out, slide across, or swing into place as partitions are also ingenious solutions, although such divisions are more permanent. For true flexibility, provide options for both openness and enclosure, thus meeting your changing needs without committing to a permanent configuration of your space.

FLEXIBILITY IS AN ESSENTIAL ELEMENT OF OPEN-PLAN LIVING

Integration

Open-plan living allows you to create a multifunctional living environment that will meet all your needs. By grouping activities into zones, you can create an efficient and enjoyable place in which to live. Yet different activities tend to overlap, so working out how best to combine different activities within zones and how to integrate zones within a single space is a complex issue.

Before making any decisions about integration, first consider the multitude of routine activities that take place in your home. Group any related activities together in one zone, or in zones that are in close proximity to each other. Position the zones according to frequency of use, ease of access and proximity to other zones. Consider the progression from public to private zones, and install flexible dividers or incorporate an intermediate cross-over area between the two.

The main challenge of integration is maintaining an intrinsic quality of openness in an interior while still making adequate provision for privacy and reclusion. Striking this balance is a key factor in determining how comfortable it is to live in an open-plan home, especially if you are part of a busy family unit with people of all ages sharing the same space. Be aware of the day-to-day demands on your space and use dividers to screen more intimate zones, such as bathing or sleeping areas.

Often, the ideal solution is a reconciliation of what is practical, logical, and cost-efficient. Special architectural or structural features might perhaps pre-designate an area for one specific use or suggest the arrangement of a sequence of zones. The position of utilities and drains, for example, will indicate possible locations for kitchen sinks and bathtubs. Even so, with resourceful planning and possible re-routing of service systems, it is always possible to avoid over-compartmentalizing activities in a conventional way. After all, freedom, flexibility, and individual expression are the whole point of open-plan living.

opposite left
Integrating a bathing and sitting area is an unconventional arrangement. However, the orientation of this salvaged bathtub and sofa adds a degree of separation.
left Widening the existing openings, removing doors, and reducing the height of internal walls are all simple, low-key ways of improving integration between formerly separate areas in conventional domestic interiors.

this page Simple white roll-up shades diffuse incoming light from full-width windows, changing the emphasis from the external to the internal environment.
opposite At a bay window, floor-to-ceiling roll-up shades add an essential element of privacy and separation from the busy street outside without reducing light levels.

Positive assets

Converting an interior into a single space means that positive assets, such as ample daylight or a great view, are accessible throughout the space, not exclusive to one part of it.

Light enlivens and enhances everything: a plain white wall, the color and texture of fabric, the shape and line of furniture. It does not simply provide illumination, but is a vital asset that can animate a space with contrast and variation. Mapping out the direction from which light enters a space and moves around it is essential when planning structural changes to increase the amount of light in an interior or improve its distribution. This information will help you plan your space to make the most of the available light at different times of day. You may wish to position a sleeping area so you wake up to sunlight, or site a work space to take advantage of the late afternoon sun.

If they are an option, extra windows and skylights will let in extra light. Inserting a skylight in a ceiling recess will create a luminous lightwell and a dynamic architectural feature. To diffuse or modulate light in excessively bright environments, or simply to add a degree of separation between internal and external worlds, screen windows or glass walls with voile or wire mesh panels. Alternatively, install simple window shades.

One of the big advantages of living in an open-plan space is the increased general access to and visual prominence of an original or new architectural feature of special interest. In a domestic space, this is often a key architectural feature that was formerly exclusive to one room, such as original crown moldings, a decorative fireplace, or a large bay window. In an ex-industrial environment, original architectural features can act as fascinating reminders of a previous existence, and can also become an intrinsic part of a new scheme. For example, a pair of original steel loading-bay doors might inspire a utilitarian aesthetic, with rough, unfinished walls. Alternatively, a bold new architectural feature, such as a circular skylight, could become the central focus of a space.

URES ARE FASCINATING REMINDERS OF A VERY DIFFERENT PREVIOUS EXISTENCE

However, it's essential to consider the proportion and scale of the architectural features in a new open-plan environment. Some original features, such as a period fireplace, which have a powerful link to the previous interior arrangement, may look less impressive or out of place outside their original framework, consequently undermining the openness and unity of the new arrangement.

opposite above An adventurous conversion of a subterranean space maximizes the incoming light that floods in through a glass ceiling over one half of the space. As the brightest area, this is the obvious position for a relaxing zone and an internal garden.

above center and right The distinctive barrel-vaulted ceiling was the starting point for this arrangement, with a large kitchen and dining zone occupying the center of the interior and the bathing and sleeping areas arranged down one side of the space.

Change and review

For some people, open-plan living is a logical next step, representing a timely move away from conventional domestic interiors toward a more versatile, less formal living space. For others, it is a chance to explore a completely different way of living, one with a dynamic sense of freedom, space, and light.

Before committing yourself to a complete change in lifestyle, think about your circumstances and the level of change you want. Take into account any potential changes in circumstance— if your family grows, where will the new arrivals be accommodated? Also look at different one-space options. There are many different ways to embrace the philosophy of open-plan living, and not all of them require a complete rejection of everything that is familiar and recognizable.

If open-plan living represents a radical move for you, possibly from a conventional house to a loft, allow for a period of adjustment to this way of life before you undertake alterations. Everything is up for review, from how you organize and use your space to the levels of openness and sharing. Even existing furniture may require a rethink. Avoid snap decisions. Accept this as a challenge, one that requires imaginative design and planning solutions, but will ultimately lead to a more versatile and practical lifestyle.

opposite In a New York apartment, flexible curtain track and plastic sheeting separate off a sleeping area and diffuse the incoming light.

this page This expansive industrial conversion houses a series of separate yet interconnecting areas. Paper roll-up shades make versatile dividers.

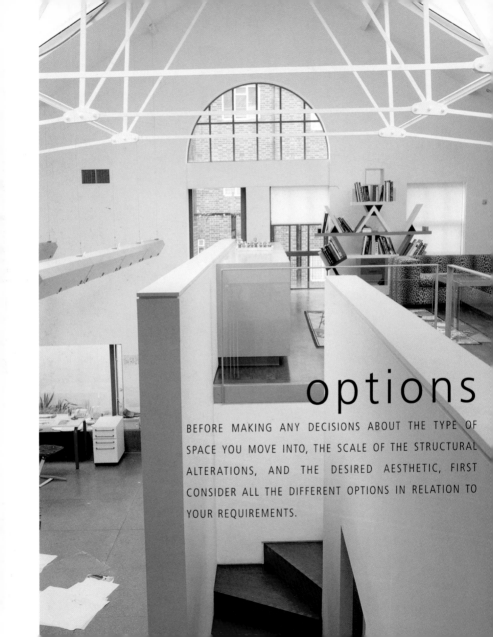

options

BEFORE MAKING ANY DECISIONS ABOUT THE TYPE OF SPACE YOU MOVE INTO, THE SCALE OF THE STRUCTURAL ALTERATIONS, AND THE DESIRED AESTHETIC, FIRST CONSIDER ALL THE DIFFERENT OPTIONS IN RELATION TO YOUR REQUIREMENTS.

Open-plan opportunities

There are essentially two different types of open-plan home—non-domestic spaces, such as ex-industrial units, or conventional properties, such as apartments and houses, which are either original open-plan spaces or have been restructured into a single space.

Non-domestic space Former light-industrial buildings often boast generous proportions and original details. They offer the opportunity to create a new and unique living environment. Although it is possible to develop such a building yourself, it is a huge job requiring frequent liaison with municipal departments regarding planning permission, change of use (from non-domestic to domestic premises), and the supply of basic utilities. A venture of this kind is a huge undertaking. Finding a non-domestic building that can be converted to a single domestic unit is a different matter, one that is well worth the time and effort involved.

Perhaps the best option is a ready-made conversion. Look for those conversions that are sympathetic to the original building, and avoid those that disregard the building and have disappointingly conventional interiors as a result. It can be difficult to find units prior to development, but some developers allow or even invite input from future purchasers. If you see a building of interest undergoing conversion, make enquiries of the builders or developer and get in on the act of conversion as soon as possible. Once original details are lost, they are gone forever.

opposite A geometric division of a former mail-sorting center provides distinct activity areas for the artist owner's studio and living space.

above right and right Many non-domestic buildings offer diverse and fascinating options for conversion to open-plan homes.

left and opposite Removing the walls of an earlier conversion restored this space to its original proportions. The capsule kitchen is a neat solution in a small space.

below left A few minor yet effective adjustments brought this space up to date to provide a compact inner-city base.

Domestic space The benefit of domestic space is its wide availability and a familiar set of references. The interior dimensions, window sizes, and ceiling heights are all relatively unchallenging. Such details can change with radical restructuring, but even the most inventive schemes cannot conceal the basic framework. And the basic framework of a domestic space is often an immediately recognizable one.

However, many domestic environments have great open-plan potential, and there are several options available, from individual houses to purpose-built apartments. One- or two-story buildings are a logical option. And while a house extending over three or four different levels is a more challenging option, it is not an unworkable one.

Some apartments built since the 1950s already exhibit a degree of open-plan living, integrating day-to-day living activities as an expression of a new informality in contemporary lifestyles. Interestingly, a 1950's apartment can impose a stricter sense of architectural correctness than a nineteenth-century house. The powerful aesthetics of 1950s, '60s, and '70s architecture can dominate a plan and inhibit a simple rationalization of the space.

Since many older homes have been split into a series of smaller units, returning an apartment to a single space often restores an interior's original dimensions and reinstates a sense of proportion and light. Windows regain their correct position and light can flow through an interior without the interruption of numerous partition walls.

opposite and far left Transporting the side of a container truck into a former commercial space in New York introduces a powerful industrial aesthetic and divides the space into public and private areas. **left** The effect of using industrial elements like over-size ducting is decorative as well as functional.

New aesthetics

Choosing an aesthetic or interior style for your open-plan space—whether it is raw and industrial or a sleek design with high-spec finishes—will help you to direct every design and planning decision toward a consistent concept. Ideally, consider the aesthetics at the very beginning of a project. Knowing exactly how you want a space to look will provide a vital reference when you are choosing flooring and wall finishes, as well as deciding on how to divide space and what type of fixtures to install. In this way, the aesthetic is an integral part of a space, not a decorative add-on

An interior style that takes the original architecture of a building as the starting point for the plan will bring visual definition to a space in a direct and unpretentious way. Conversely, imposing a random aesthetic that has no link to the architecture of a space, unless it is used to present a dynamic and consistent juxtaposition to the interior, will only detract and distract from any sense of unity. This is not a caution against introducing color, comfort, or possessions. All these elements can bring a strong new identity to an interior. However, it is a caution against an assortment of discordant elements that do not fit together and will diminish an overall sense of space or visual simplicity.

With ex-industrial buildings, such as factories and workshops, a raw, hard-edged aesthetic is in keeping with the original architecture as well as any remaining structural details or industrial elements in the space. Retaining original features is a way of acknowledging the past existence of a space, too. Obliterating any sense of a building's

IDEALLY, YOU SHOULD CONSIDER THE AESTHETICS OF THE SPACE AT THE VERY BEGINNING OF A PROJECT, NOT AT THE END heritage or original purpose by overlayering every surface with a glossy new finish is a mistake. In a compact interior, where a sense of space is a key consideration, a minimal, pared-down aesthetic will streamline an interior and optimize space. If this style is to work, orderliness, tidiness, and attention to detail are of paramount importance. Vigilance is everything. Edit your possessions and eliminate any redundant items. Clutter or excess furniture will only diminish a sense of space.

Stylistic contrasts between the architecture of a space and its contents can add a sense of excitement to a scheme by introducing a degree of friction. Exposed industrial or structural elements and modern upholstered furniture is an interesting combination. Keep to simple, sculptural shapes and a precise symmetrical arrangement of furniture.

Classical domestic architecture often suggests a traditional interior. However, reconfiguring such a space into an open-plan environment equipped with industrial fixtures will enliven it with an unexpected element of contradiction. The juxtaposition will be particularly effective if you keep the structural elements and contents apart. Minimize the connections between the two by introducing freestanding fixtures and furniture.

right The former living room of a large period townhouse was converted into a small open-plan apartment. To create a feeling of space and light, the interior has been stripped of all its traditional decorative features, leaving instead a pared-down, minimalist shell.

left Although this space is devoid of decorative objects, the overall design and mix of wood, marble, glass, steel, and different planes of white create a visually stimulating yet orderly environment.

above In a voluminous New York loft, white ceilings and walls and a smooth concrete floor provide a low-key backdrop to a mix of furniture and artefacts with an Eastern influence.

Structural change

Imaginative planning and design can bring about dramatic spatial transformations and result in the best possible use of the available space and light in an interior. Less radical yet equally inspirational schemes can reorganize space in a way that will provide an efficient framework for living that suits current requirements, while still retaining a degree of flexibility to accommodate future change.

With any level of structural change, it is essential to be aware of code restrictions and to follow any regulations. This is particularly the case with units in a block, historic houses and buildings of special architectural interest, or if you want to make changes to the exterior of a building. If you remove a structural or load-bearing wall, it is necessary to add a concrete, metal, or timber beam to support the opening. The size of the beam depends on how much weight it must support. Knocking through new openings, adding mezzanine levels, or removing part of the floor may all require additional support. Some non-domestic buildings can tolerate alterations without additional strengthening. However, it is essential to check with relevant planning departments, a surveyor, or a structural engineer before undertaking structural alterations. And even the simplest structural changes may also require changes to utilities and service systems. They may also be subject to regulations, so seek professional advice about any alterations.

opposite, above and above right This bold conversion of a former schoolhouse sensitively juxtaposes new and original features to create a bold and dynamic contemporary environment. The lower floor is a spacious living area with staircases leading to mezzanine levels at each end.

Assessment and action

Whether you are contemplating low-level alterations or radical change, assessing your requirements is the first step.

The main issues to consider are how best to use the available space, how to integrate several different activity zones, and how to give visual definition to the whole interior. Whether you live as a singleton, a couple, or a family, taking into account everyone's requirements is a complex process. Yet it will provide you with essential information and indicate any areas that are in need of change or improvement. It will also focus time, effort, and creativity on finding workable, economical solutions.

Begin by listing all the different ways in which you use your space. Run through the events of a typical weekday and weekend, and list every activity that takes place in your home. Which activities are public or social? Which activities require privacy or isolation? Do conflicts of interest arise as a result of different activities? If you have young children, make two lists for every child, one that covers the child's current requirements, and one that covers the child's requirements five years from now. All this information will indicate ways in which you can organize and combine activities, with different degrees of privacy and openness. It will also provide an essential checklist for any planning or design decisions. Make use of it to keep changes and developments moving in the right direction, in line with your expectations.

opposite left Floor-to-ceiling paper shades screen off a work area tucked away in a corner and separate it from the main body of the space.
opposite right If cooking and eating are key activities in your home, position the kitchen at the center of your space. This kitchen's vibrant color signals its important role.
this page This sleeping area strikes a comfortable balance between connection with the living area and a sense of privacy.

BEFORE YOU MAKE ANY FINAL DECISIONS, TAKE TIME TO INVESTIGATE EVERY OPTION

Now that you know exactly what you need from your space, assess it as it currently exists. Include any positive or negative observations. Look objectively at the volume and dimensions. Draw a rough floorplan and note the general layout and the position of the facilities and utilities. Map out the circulation routes around the space and note any areas of congestion or inconvenient restrictions. Chart the way that light enters and moves around the space, indicating the different areas it animates at different times of day.

Finally, you can review all the information about your current and future requirements together with your observations about the space. Before you make any final decisions, take time to ponder on all the possible improvements, to discuss and review your ideas in depth, and to investigate every option.

Now is the time to set your budget, investigate any restrictions to possible changes, and decide on acceptable levels of disruption and time limits. If you are contemplating large-scale structural changes, a major reorganization of space, or changes to the existing utilities, this is the moment to bring in the professionals for expert advice and creative input.

The end result of analyzing every aspect of a project in this way is a clear objective and a precise step-by-step plan of action. Regardless of the level of change you are planning, your aim is to find the most practical and economical way ahead. Employing builders, beginning work, and then changing tack will increase costs considerably. If at all possible, avoid making any changes to your plans once work has begun and is underway. It will save you money and prevent any potential delays, as well as helping you maintain a good working relationship with your builders.

left A light-industrial space is given an inexpensive makeover with white paint and clever structural add-ons, including a diagonal division between living and working areas and a step up to a sleeping zone. The result is a simple, comfortable space with a welcoming sense of space and light.

help

FOR COMPLEX PROJECTS OR ALTERATIONS THAT AFFECT THE
BASIC STRUCTURE OF THE SERVICES IN A PROPERTY, SOME
FORM OF SPECIALIZED GUIDANCE IS ESSENTIAL.

Architects, surveyors, engineers, and builders

Most projects break down into three stages: planning and design, administration and supervision (checking building regulations and applying for planning permissions), and the actual building work. For extensive and complex projects, it is important to employ professionals to design, plan, and manage the work. For less complex alterations, it is possible to involve experts in only certain aspects of the job—to employ an architect to design and plan the project without overseeing the work, for example.

opposite and above In a conventional domestic interior it is not always possible to remove walls or radically reconfigure space. Simple devices like inserting internal windows and widening existing openings can transform a space and introduce a new sense of connection.

Architects An architect brings vision and experience to a project, guaranteeing the best possible result in terms of creativity and cost-efficiency. As well as planning and design, an architect can suggest materials, find specialized contractors or manufacturers to provide fixtures and fittings, and recommend a good builder. The basis of a good working relationship is trust, communication, and confidence, so meet and talk to architects whose work you like, or ask friends for recommendations. Ask to see photos of recent projects, or visit them yourself.

Chartered surveyors Chartered surveyors offer advice on all aspects of buying and selling property. If you are contemplating buying a property or making structural changes to your current property, a survey will provide essential information about the condition of the building. It will point out any defects, which may influence your decision to buy, or indicate areas that are in need of improvement and development.

Structural engineers Structural engineers will assess a building's structure and stability. Areas for consideration include the foundations, walls, columns, beams, and roof components. A structural engineer can specify materials, prepare technical drawings, check regulations and restrictions, and obtain relevant consents and permissions, prepare costings, and monitor the actual building work.

Builders The best option for finding a builder is personal recommendation. If you are employing an architect or a structural engineer, they may be able to suggest builders to undertake your project. Alternatively, trade associations can recommend local builders. Be precise about your requirements—prepare a detailed written brief and ask the builder for a written estimate.

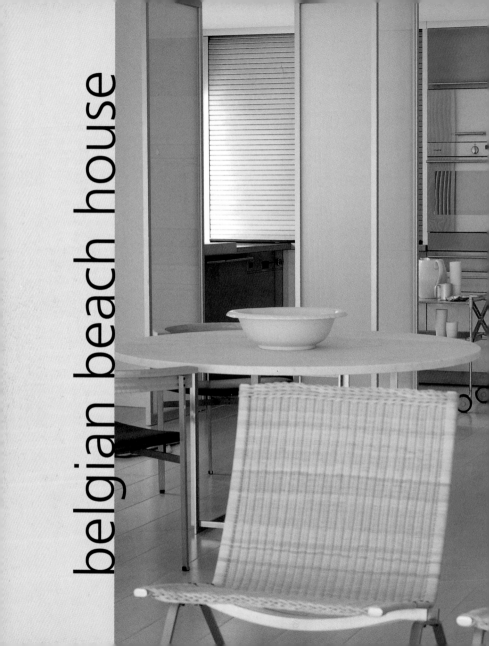

belgian beach house

SPACIOUS SEASIDE APARTMENT

This radical transformation of a contemporary yet conventional weekend home in a coastal town in Belgium allows the owners maximum flexibility. The new open-plan scheme significantly improves the use of space, the light distribution, and access to sea views. Now a translucent environment with a sense of spaciousness that is entirely in keeping with its location, the apartment offers a refreshing escape from urban life.

In an ideal location overlooking the ocean, this apartment is a long rectangular space that runs the full length of an uninspiring purpose-built building, with expansive windows and outdoor terraces at each end. Standard windows ranged down one side of the space look out onto an identical building next door. The original interior—an unimaginative domestic layout with poor light distribution and restricted sea views—did not optimize the positive assets of the space.

The architects' new plan comprises large open areas at both ends of the apartment, which make excellent use of the wonderful light and views. At the front of the apartment, a spacious living, dining, and kitchen area overlooks the sea, while at the back, the tranquil sleeping area faces inward toward the town. A sequence of individual work, storage, shower, and bathing areas are lined up in between, connecting the two ends of the apartment.

Large moving panels of opaque glass and wood provide multiple possibilities for opening or enclosing every area and for subdividing the space as a whole.

floor plan This modern apartment consists of a long, thin rectangular space with large windows at either end and all along one outside wall. Versatile sliding panels divide the front and back of the apartment into two zones, public and private, with additional smaller subdivisions for working, bathing, and storage areas neatly sandwiched in between.

sleeping

bathing

bathing

working

cooking

relaxing

dining

opposite inset above and center The kitchen area is a series of flexible divisions, from the stainless steel shutters that screen the work surface to the movable glass panels that enclose it.

this page A corridor running the length of the apartment links the sleeping and living areas. Wood or glass panels slide across the corridor to create a sense of separation.

A wooden panel that slides across the corridor divides the apartment into two sections, while a glass panel in a similar position offers a very different degree of separation. The moving panels underline and facilitate the architects' intention to provide flexible, optional divisions between a front-of-house area and the back-of-house facilities. And while the new organization of space retains an element of the original layout, with the sitting and kitchen areas on the water side of the apartment and sleeping and bathing on the town side, the experience of being in the space is radically different.

Surrounding the kitchen area with glass panels continues the principle of flexibility. When closed, the panels create an opaque box, rather like an abstract art installation. As the panels open or slide across, the area reconfigures, and the sightlines from and access to the kitchen change. Four independent panels facing the ocean pivot in or out in multiple variations, reflecting

opposite left The sleeping area is a secondary relaxing zone, with inviting furniture, a television, and several different lighting options.
far left The living room is tranquil and inviting, complete with natural light, soft seating, and a low table for drinks or books.
left A desk set into a narrow alcove provides a useful work space.

and refracting light with their every movement. Each glass panel projects monochromatic images and shadows, enlivening the space with a new landscape and extra dimensions.

Other reflective surfaces throughout the space catch and throw back light and shadows with similar effect. The sycamore flooring running from front to back (except in the shower and bathing areas), the stainless steel kitchen counters, equipment, and shuttering, and the expansive mirrors all contribute to an effect of luminosity and a special quality of light.

White window shades at every window moderate the light, reduce glare, and maintain a temperate environment. Changing the position of the shades also alters the focus of the space. With the shades down, the light is diffused and a sense of enclosure is created. When the shades are up, revealing views of the ever-changing sea and sky, there is a sense of exposure to the elements and connection with the world outside.

zoning

relaxing **I** cooking **I** bathing **I** sleeping **I** working

ORGANIZING AN OPEN-PLAN ENVIRONMENT IS ABOUT COMBINING DIFFERENT ACTIVITIES INTO A LOGICAL SEQUENCE OF INTERCONNECTING ZONES. DESIGNATING A WELL-LIT, OPEN AREA AS A RELAXING ZONE WILL PROVIDE A WELCOMING ENVIRONMENT, SOMEWHERE TO BE AT EASE WITH FAMILY AND FRIENDS.

relaxing

An open-plan interior incorporates many different activities, and dividing these activities into zones facilitates good organization and the optimum use of space. Few zones are dedicated to a single activity—the majority combine several related activities, such as cooking and eating, or reading and listening to music. Unlike a conventional domestic environment, which has set divisions between different zones, an open-plan environment is about flexibility and integration. So the way a zone relates to the general space is just as important as the way it functions in its own right.

There's no set formula for organizing zones within a space—everyone has different requirements and every space will suggest a different solution. Obviously, it makes sense to take advantage of well-lit areas for relaxing, eating, and cooking zones, but the amount of space devoted to each activity is a matter of individual preference. It's important to assess your personal requirements and structure the main

opposite In a light, open workshop conversion, a high-level storage panel in the kitchen area separates front-of-house and back-of-house activities.

left A sliding panel is an ingenious flexible storage solution for a multi-functional relaxing zone and brings vibrant color to a light, white space.

living area to suit your lifestyle. If you enjoy social activities such as entertaining, this suggests one way to organize your space. If you enjoy more solitary pursuits, such as listening to music, this suggests a different arrangement.

In a multifunctional relaxing zone, where many activities coexist and overlap, a flexible arrangement of furniture, storage, and lighting is essential. The style and position of furniture and the lighting effects will define and facilitate everyday use and enjoyment of the zone.

When choosing furniture, consider the scale and architecture of your interior. In an expansive loft, for example, a geometric arrangement of big sofas and

a central low table will anchor a relaxing zone. Soft textures and shapes can provide an interesting juxtaposition with industrial concrete flooring or other non-domestic details. In smaller spaces, beware of allowing oversized pieces to dominate the space, as they may compromise the overall flexibility and versatility of the zone.

A configuration of chairs is often the main indicator of a relaxing zone, establishing a general style and indicating the level of informality. Different chairs fit different activities, so aim to provide a selection of soft (easy) and hard (upright) seating to meet your requirements and to define different activities. For example,

opposite left A fabric tent defines an intimate alternative seating arrangement for breakfast and afternoon tea.
opposite right, above and below Simple sheer drapes diffuse the sunlight and provide semi-transparent dividers between public and private areas.
this page The classic style and formal arrangement of this table and chairs contrasts with the raw structure of a New York loft space.

group armchairs together for general conversation, position a recliner on its own for quiet reading, and gather upright chairs together around a table for eating. Sofas often end up as a big seat for one person, so don't feel you should automatically include one. If you enjoy putting your feet up, a chaise longue or daybed may be a better option, as they take up less space and are often more comfortable. On a practical note, single chairs are easier to move and reconfigure into different seating arrangements and therefore are more versatile.

A selection of stools and storage cubes offer space-efficient supplementary seating—ideal for the occasional influx of people—and also function as side tables

this page In a typical multifunctional living space, arrangements of furniture and lighting suggest different activities. A classic sofa, low table, and task lighting provide a comfortable place for reading and relaxing.

opposite far left
In an open-plan
apartment, a table
and chairs in a quiet
setting by a window
provide an
alternative to the
main dining table.
above A narrow
lobby off the main
living space is
furnished with easy
chairs and a rug to
provide an informal
seating area.

for the phone, a pile of books, or a coffee cup. Floor cushions
add an informal note, as well as providing child-friendly seating
options. A bed is an inexpensive alternative to chairs. It can
provide a comfortable communal seating area and works well in
either a big space or a small studio. Choose a bed base on
wheels for maximum flexibility, and throw on a cover to protect
and conceal pillows and comforters. Store bed linen elsewhere
or, if the bed is high enough, in comforters beneath it. Some
divans come with built-in storage space in the base.

Accessible and flexible storage solutions will help create a
sense of organization and maintain a sense of space. Books,
television sets, CD players, CDs, DVD players, DVDs, board and
computer games all require shelf space. Finding a place for
everything is a challenge, but designing and putting together

efficient storage will go a long way toward preventing chaos. However, if everything is hidden from view, an area can look austere. Strike a balance— display favorite items and store the rest out of sight.

Mobile trolleys are a big bonus in an open-plan environment, enabling you to move heavy pieces of entertainment equipment around easily and relocate them when they are not in use. For example, you can push a large-screen television into a central area for viewing then wheel it out of sight afterward.

Some storage solutions take advantage of the structure of a space to provide inventive options. Fitting a bookcase into a narrow recess makes use of an otherwise empty space and provides unobtrusive storage. Make the

most of alcoves or recesses by using them to house storage units or display space.

Creative lighting is an important factor in a relaxing zone. Different combinations of lights signal different moods, from bright and upbeat to low-key and intimate. Subtle ambient lighting is ideal for relaxing and entertaining, and a central fixture on a dimmer switch can deliver this effect. Accent lighting enlivens an environment by introducing contrasting areas of light and shade, while task lighting directs a pool of light to illuminate a specific activity. Lighting design is a complex issue. If you plan to install a new lighting system, consult an expert. However, investing in floor lamps to supplement a central fixture and wall lights will provide scope for many different combinations.

this page An expansive double-height window in a New York loft is a compelling backdrop to a comfortable seating area.

london purpose-built

CASE STUDY 2

MODERN CITY APARTMENT

This compact apartment is only a few minutes' walk from the owner's design studio. A strong architectural aesthetic combined with the convenience of a buzzing inner-city location makes this small space an inspiring base. Ingenious alterations have successfully updated the space by acknowledging the spirit of the original concept without creating a set piece of design history.

This small apartment, one of a series of open-plan single or double occupancy units, is situated on the top floor of a low-rise building in an inner-city location. The block is part of a 1950's public-housing complex originally built for local blue-collar professionals such as nurses and the police.

With a heritage listing to protect the existing space and limit any changes, acknowledging and understanding the history of the apartment is an important part of the owner/occupier package and adds to the excitement of living here—even though regulations and restrictions can sometimes protect the wrong thing, like an unauthentic replacement kitchen. So while the owner's ambition is restoration, even returning the kitchen to something like its original simplicity now requires planning permission.

The apartment's full-width arched window and barrel-shaped ceiling are exclusive to the top-floor units in the building and contribute to the high levels of light and general sense of space. The

wall of glass outlines a panoramic view
over east London. This view, and the
overall impression of luminosity and
space, are the first things that strike you
upon entering the apartment, drawing
the eye straight past the kitchen area,
which is set to one side of the entrance,
and into the main living area beyond.

Seventy percent of the space is
occupied by a living area that contains
different seating configurations that
define different activities. There are chairs
arranged around a table for eating or

**this page and
opposite** The view
from the entrance
shows the kitchen
area at the left,
sitting area directly
ahead, and the
sleeping area to
the right.

floor plan The apartment is a compact rectangle, with a glass wall in front of the relaxing zone. Attention to detail on the part of the original architects means that there are several storage solutions built into the kichen and relaxing areas—vital in a space of this size.

working, chairs positioned for contemplating the view from the window, and a group configuration with a sofa for conversation and socializing. A solitary lounger, reading light, and occasional table together with a large collection of design and photographic books signal the key area of interest and activity. The simple storage system for books is one of the new additions to the space. Running the full length of the living area, the shelving provides an ingenious opportunity for both storage and display.

In full view from the lounger, the sleeping zone is an open box set one step up from the main living area. The change in level, the wall panel intersecting the storage unit, and the chain curtain are all new additions. The wall and the chain divider provide an ingenious division between areas without compromising the ease of transition or challenging the sense of overall openness. They underline what is remarkable about this compact space. Different areas interconnect in a logical sequence, yet also manage to convey a sense of independence and change in style specific to their different functions.

left Hanging a simple chain-link curtain across the opening between the main sitting area and the sleeping zone provides an inventive but effective screen that provides some privacy but retains a sense of openness.

above left An inexpensive shelving tower provides storage for shirts and other clothing. Castors have been attached to the base, so it can be spun around to face the wall, leaving a single neat shelf on view.

WITH RESOURCEFUL PLANNING, IT IS POSSIBLE TO
DESIGN A HIGH-PERFORMANCE, USER-FRIENDLY
KITCHEN AREA. CLEVER DIVIDERS AND WELL-
THOUGHT-OUT STORAGE WILL ADD FLEXIBILITY
AND VERSATILITY, AND FACILITATE INTEGRATION
WITH THE REST OF YOUR SPACE.

cooking

When planning and designing a kitchen area, think about its
frequency of use, ease of access, and its position in your interior.
Look at the relationship between cooking and eating. Do you
cook every day or do you simply use the kitchen to heat up
ready-made meals? How many people does the kitchen cater
for? The size and prominence of a kitchen area should reflect its
role in your day-to-day life. So be realistic in your evaluation –
getting it wrong and overstating or underplaying a kitchen area
is a waste of an opportunity, effort, and space.

Before you decide to rearrange your space to accommodate
a new kitchen area or change around an existing installation,
check the utilities and services. Water supplies and drainage are
essential services that may need access to external walls. It may

above left and center
Precision fixtures, like
these high-specification
stainless steel units,
utensils, and
countertops, create
a minimalist look.
above A capsule
kitchen hides behind
retractable doors.
opposite In a city
apartment used for
weekend breaks, the
compact kitchen-in-
a-cupboard is exactly
the right size for use.

above top and bottom Clever ideas like installing an oven in the end of a table and slotting a fridge under steps to a mezzanine level maximize space in a compact and minimalist kitchen area.

above Long wooden benches, which can be neatly tucked away under the table when not in use, are a space-saving seating solution that is ideally suited to this simple and clutter-free cooking zone.

opposite Integrating a high-specification food preparation area (complete with two-burner cooktop and a kitchen sink) with a dining table, makes use of all the available space in a kitchen.

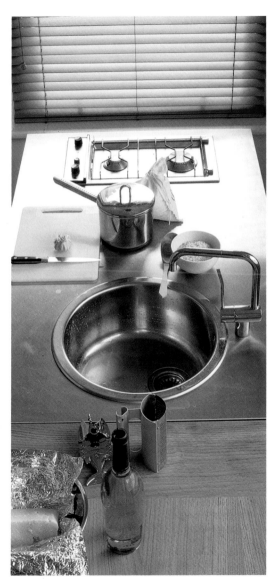

be possible to update or extend existing systems to allow a change in position of a kitchen area, although if a system is deficient or out of date, a complete refit is the best option. Drainage and waste pipes require a minimum gradient, so position sinks, dishwashers, and washing machines within reasonable distance of an external outlet. Plan new piping with as few twists and bends as possible, to reduce the risk of blockages.

Good ventilation removes excess moisture from the atmosphere and prevents cooking smells from invading the rest of the space (this is a sensible precaution if, for example, clothes are kept in an open storage system). Open windows go a long way to keep fresh air circulating, yet high-specification cooking equipment can produce excessive amounts of moisture that will eventually damage the fabric of an environment. And while smell is a powerful and vital stimulant in the preparation, cooking, and eating process, the lingering smell of yesterday's food is not quite as appealing. However, a quick session with an extractor fan will soon clear the air. For direct effect, install a cooking hood above cooking equipment or, to provide good general ventilation, fit extractor fans in walls and windows.

Orientation is an important factor within the kitchen area itself and affects its integration with the overall space. For example, installing a low-level line of units along an outside wall, possibly with a window with a pleasant view, focuses a kitchen area, and anyone working in it, away from the rest of the space. Standing at the work-surface preparing food or cooking will involve turning your back on everything else. If you like to work away from any distraction, possibly in isolation, then this is a good option.

Putting an identical arrangement of low-level units away from the wall, with access from both sides so people can walk around the unit, will transform the orientation of your kitchen area and the experience of being in it. If you live with young children who need your attention, or like cooking to be a social event, this is a practical arrangement. Likewise, dividing a kitchen into two parallel lines of units, or locating everything in a central unit or block, will involve different movements around the kitchen area and create different connections with the overall space.

this picture Parallel high- and low-level cabinets accommodate an efficient kitchen with easy access to the ample storage space.

opposite Providing a place to sit, like these stools attached to the end of a countertop, signal the kitchen area as a social place.
below Sockets set flush in a countertop facilitate efficiency and avoid the hazard of trailing cords.

below Two sliding panels at the end of this functional galley kitchen area provide varying degrees of separation from the rest of the space and modulate the flow of light.

opposite above In a converted former schoolhouse, the compact kitchen area is slotted in beneath a mezzanine level and overlooks a double-height eating and relaxing zone.

opposite below Flat panels flip down to conceal the work surfaces and the food preparation area, while a roll-up shade between the kitchen and eating areas screens mess.

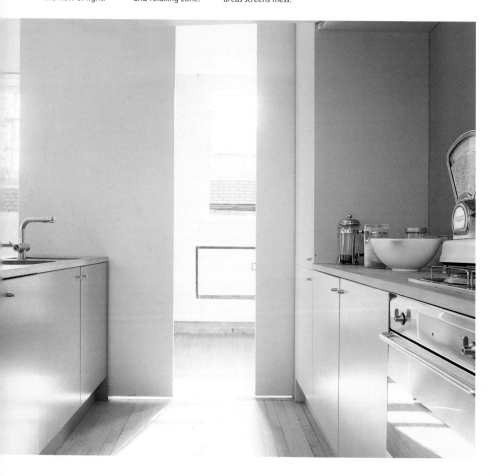

If your kitchen area is also intended to be a social place, take this into account in the planning and design. Include broad work surfaces with access from both sides, and put stools around a work surface to encourage people to participate or spectate. However, it's important to pay attention to safety issues. Do not invite people to sit next to a hazardous hot surface. Keep seating away from the main work triangle between cooking unit, sink, and work surface. And for general efficiency and safety, incorporate heatproof surfaces alongside cooking units, so the cook can avoid walking around with hot pots and pans. Ideally, provide somewhere comfortable so that guests or family can sit close by, but away from the general work traffic. A sense of openness, easy access, and light will promote the kitchen area as a friendly, welcoming environment.

Apart from installing a cooking unit and plumbing in a kitchen sink, there is no reason to permanently fix anything else in one place. Mobile work surfaces, kitchen tables, and storage units will all add versatility to a kitchen area and make your working environment responsive to your changing requirements. Even in a compact kitchen area, including a single unit on wheels and storing it out of the way under a work surface or in a built-in cupboard will increase overall flexibility.

Creating a kitchen with different, varying levels of enclosure and openness increases flexibility and versatility. Simple ideas like a pull-down shutter or sliding screen to enclose a cooking unit can shift the focus of a kitchen area away from the function of preparing large family meals to simple low-key activities like making a single cup of coffee. This change in emphasis and appearance introduces new possibilities for use, changing the dynamic from that of a hard-working area to a more low-key and informal one. Alternatively, it's possible to use lighting to transfer emphasis from one activity area to another.

Streamlining the industrial elements of a kitchen area into a single panel or unit can add efficiency and visual simplicity to an arrangement. Planning a kitchen area as a series of logical and ergonomic workstations, perhaps with one low-level and one high-level unit, will optimize the available space. One

left and below In a remarkably compact kitchen area, a glass panel set over the stairwell is a clever idea that allows light to reach the staircase and also creates another work surface. Open shelves provide extra storage space.

solution to a small space is to integrate cooking and eating areas into a single central workbench, with an oven and cooktop built in at one end and a separate storage unit elsewhere. This approach does not preclude display and open storage, which can add vitality and individuality to an area, but it is a caution against overcrowding or clutter.

Keep an open mind about the layout and aesthetics of a kitchen until you have finalized the location and structure. While thinking about how you will organize the area is a critical part of the decision-making process, setting your heart on an industrial aesthetic, for example, with stainless steel equipment and work-surfaces, may not be the best solution for integrating the area into the rest of your space. Sometimes the best option is a compromise of aesthetics, cost-efficiency, and practicality. An efficient plan that makes good use of space is far preferable to an unworkable or over-complex arrangement of set pieces.

Choose fixtures and equipment that are compatible with the scale and general style of the interior. Standard fixtures and appliances can look out of scale in a loft space—this type of environment offers an opportunity to use bold architectural statements and unconventional elements, such as concrete work-surfaces and industrial-style lighting. In a compact interior, choose sleek precision elements to maximize the available space. Slim dishwashers and washing machines offer useful alternatives to standard-width equipment and can make all the difference between an efficient area and a labor-intensive one.

this page Open shelving in front of a window creates storage space for pots and pans and adds a bold visual focus in a compact kitchen.

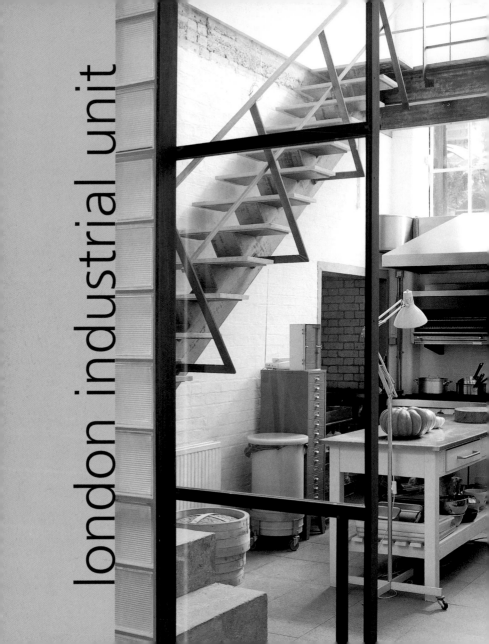

london industrial unit

Converting a raw industrial unit to domestic use is an exciting opportunity to devise an entirely original and individual place to live. Taking on a project of this size and complexity, coordinating and designing every aspect personally without any previous experience, and producing such an uncompromisingly modern result, as the owner of this space did, is a triumph of vision and determination.

top left and above left Many of the kitchen appliances are ex-industrial. The anglepoise lamps are old hospital fixtures and bring a stark aesthetic to the food-preparation area.

top right and above right Everyday items such as bowls, utensils, pots, and pans are kept close at hand on old catering carts. **right** A section of the upper floor was cut out to provide access and light to the lower level of the apartment, making it possible to stand in the living area and peer over the banisters into the kitchen area below.

This exceptional apartment was once part of a printing factory in London's East End. The owner bought an empty space on two levels with no existing connections, just rough concrete floors, bare brick walls, large windows on the upper level, inadequate light on the lower level, and no basic utilities. Now, after conversion, this industrial unit is now a unique home and work space for the owner, a food writer and art director, and his partner. Given the professional food angle, the style and position of the kitchen is a big factor in the scheme of things.

Initial plans sited the kitchen area on the upper level, at the end of the main living space alongside the original loading-bay doors, to allow street-level access after food shopping. However, the owner decided against installing a kitchen in full view of the main living area, where it would be the visual focus of the space, instead allocating it a key position of power and significance on the lower level. After a radical spatial reworking, including the removal of part of the floor on the upper level and the insertion of a glass walkway and connecting stairway to the lower level, the kitchen is the new center of the space, with all the other areas radiating out from this core.

The kitchen area embodies the industrial aesthetic running throughout the apartments. It is all steel and concrete, with a battery of expensive professional catering equipment built in alongside more eclectic freestanding secondhand finds and salvaged pieces. Despite the absence of color, except during food preparation, it is still a vibrant and visually stimulating area. When viewed from the gallery in the main living area above, the kitchen looks welcoming yet low-key.

An external door at the top of a flight of stairs from the basement, one of four separate entrances to the unit, provides access after food shopping trips. Other hidden assets tucked away behind the kitchen area include structural alcoves and cavelike storage spaces that provide a generous pantry and scullery. Small-scale areas like these offset the expansiveness of the general space and add an essential element of intimacy.

The sleeping area is screened from the kitchen by a glass dividing wall and sliding clear glass panel. And beyond the sleeping area, behind a wooden panel, are a bathroom and shower. Here again, witty juxtapositions add vitality to the plan. High-specification fixtures like underfloor heating and wall-to-wall mosaic tiling coexist with salvaged bath faucets and radiators, and project an air of relaxed urban sophistication.

Up the open steel and plywood stairs and via a glass walkway lit from below is the main living area. The horizontal lines of the long, low, pale sofas and fireplace emphasize the unusual height and scale of the area. A length of tracing paper hanging from a thin metal rod in front of the original loading-bay doors conceals an original yet unpopular architectural feature. The paper diffuses light, reduces the view of a construction site opposite, and screens the interior from passers-by.

Except for the mosaic tiles in the bath and shower area, the flooring throughout the space is concrete paving slabs. Three applications of sealant were applied to protect the highly absorbent surface. High-spec underfloor heating takes the chill off this modest element— yet another juxtaposition of exclusive and low-budget elements in this dramatic and unpretentious conversion.

right The plump outlines of second-hand sofas offset the new, more elemental concrete floors and walls, and present a new interpretation of the traditional living area.

dining

working

relaxing

utilities

sleeping

bathing

storage

cooking

floor plan The apartment is situated on two levels, with part of the upper level cut away to allow light and access to the basement level. Cast concrete steps with plywood treads connect the two different levels and lead, via a glass walkway, from the tranquil sitting area down into the kitchen zone

opposite above left In keeping with the industrial aesthetic, a sheet of mirror leans up against the back of the iroko wood divider between the bathing and sleeping areas.

opposite above right Unlike standard bathroom fixtures, the scale and functional design of hospital faucets fits perfectly with the dimensions of an industrial conversion.

opposite below left and right The monumental panel of iroko wood that divides the sleeping and bathing areas is also a headboard for the bed. The deep tones of the wood provides a dramatic contrast to the blue mosaic tiles that line the bathing zone beyond.

right The bathing area incorporates a number of salvaged fixtures, yet the light and space, and warmth from underfloor heating, create an underlying sense of luxury.

below Sliding panels of textured glass divide an informal family bathing zone from a sleeping area. **below right** A solid panel that is housed in a recess in the wall can be swung across the corridor to divide the public and private areas of a loft apartment. **opposite** A bold combination of strong colors, textures, and shapes enlivens this spacious communal bathing area in a New York loft.

COMMUNAL OR SEPARATE, COLORFUL OR LOW-KEY, HIGH-TECH OR FUNCTIONAL—PLANNING A SUCCESSFUL BATHING AREA IS ALL ABOUT FINDING A SOLUTION THAT OPTIMIZES THE AVAILABLE SPACE AND FITS IN WITH YOUR LIFESTYLE.

bathing

A bathing area is a place where you are naked and accordingly at your most vulnerable. Consider how you feel about this in terms of providing an open or communal bathing area—it is likely that some degree of enclosure and separation is an essential practical concession. If communal bathing and showering is acceptable to you and your family, yet the toilet is one area requiring enclosure, then design and plan your bathing zone accordingly, or provide a separate john in a different location. Direct access to a toilet is preferable to walking past the bathtub or through a shower room.

opposite A sculptural, curving wall screens a tiny bathing zone. Access to the shower is by the window, while at the opposite end of the wall is the door to a separate toilet.
above A wall of waterproof plaster curls around the tiny shower area and screens it from the main sleeping area without separating the two zones.

If you share a bathing zone, especially with young children, consider the many different requirements and schedules that will govern its use. In a family, mornings are often the rush hour. Everyone is showering or brushing teeth together or in quick succession. Providing an extra shower room will reduce congestion. Even if you live alone, there will be times when guests are staying and competing with you for the facilities. A separate toilet is useful if your bathing and sleeping zones are integrated, since it provides somewhere for visitors to use and directs general traffic away from a potentially private area.

It is logical to integrate sleeping and bathing zones in some way and provide a sense of division or separation from the rest of your space. It's possible to divide an interior into a public front-of-house space, containing the relaxing, cooking, and eating zones, and a private back-of-house space that holds the sleeping and bathing zones. The layout of your space may naturally suggest a degree of separation—perhaps locating sleeping and bathing zones on a mezzanine level, or at one end of the space. A sliding or moving panel can reinforce this sense of division as well as providing privacy, reducing noise, and maintaining a comfortable and constant temperature.

Creating a solid division between public and private zones, possibly a wood or plasterboard sliding or fixed panel, demarcates space effectively. A division of this kind provides an opportunity for greater freedom and openness in planning and designing sleeping and bathing zones. For a family, this option also presents an opportunity to have a more informal private zone layout with communal relaxation and play areas.

Glass screens and sliding doors fit well with the functional aspect of bathing zones. Opaque or textured glass makes an ideal divider between sleeping and bathing areas and offers the advantage of privacy and enclosure without the disadvantage of blocking light. Be warned that opaque glass is less opaque when wet, so condensation and shower spray will affect its transparency. Also, it is less effective as a screen if it is in close proximity to whatever it is screening. However, for wonderful light diffusion and pure luminosity it is worth making a few

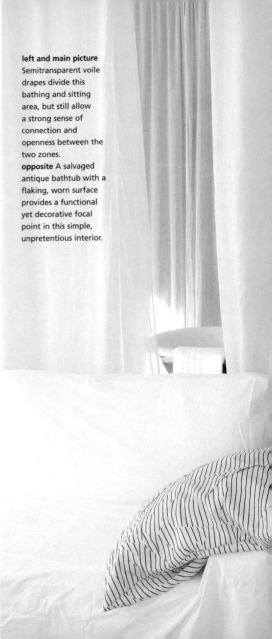

left and main picture Semitransparent voile drapes divide this bathing and sitting area, but still allow a strong sense of connection and openness between the two zones.
opposite A salvaged antique bathtub with a flaking, worn surface provides a functional yet decorative focal point in this simple, unpretentious interior.

exceptions. Sheer fabric dividers like voile provide an inexpensive and atmospheric enclosure for a bathtub and define a place for relaxation. Warmth and low-key lighting will aid this essential process. Position a tub beside a window for a view of trees and sky. Or use candles to counterbalance a functional aesthetic and change the dynamic of a space. Install a dimmer control on artificial lights and use low-level lighting to signal a change in pace and aid relaxation.

When choosing fixtures, take into account the structure and dimensions of a bathing zone and its overall aesthetic. For example, a space-saving minuscule shower and basin capsule will require high-specification compact fixtures that are in line with the general modern and streamlined effect. Simple and precise elements like mixer faucets, a built-in storage unit, and a rigid showerhead work well in this type of environment.

above A wall of folding panels open and close to reveal and conceal a capsule bathing area with a shower enclosure slotted beyond.

left and far left High specification fixtures optimize space in the compact shower enclosure. Horizontal bars set over a vertically hung radiator create a practical towel rod.

opposite above Make the most of high ceilings by creating platforms or mezzanine levels. Here, a sleeping platform is stacked atop a bathing area.

opposite below Tucked in beneath the sleeping platform, this small bathroom has no direct source of light, so relies on a glazed internal window to increase light levels.

At the opposite end of the scale, a conversion of a former industrial space with raw brickwork and surface piping requires bold and generous fixtures and appliances that are in keeping with the utilitarian aesthetic. A concrete tub with mosaic tiling and a huge salvaged showerhead that projects water onto a sloping floor are appropriate choices, in proportion with the original industrial fixtures throughout the space.

Unconventional fixtures can provide unpretentious and inexpensive alternatives to standard products. Laboratory or hospital faucets, basins, and medicine cabinets create a strong effect and guarantee reliable, long-term performance. Retail display or hotel fixtures, such as combination hooks for clothing, extending rods, and metal shelving, offer hard-working storage for accessories and towels. Commercial kitchen suppliers offer lots of inspiration and inexpensive products. Stainless steel sinks, ceramic hand-basins for professional kitchens, and metal and plastic storage bins all transfer easily into a domestic bathing zone.

If you plan to use standard fixtures, opt for simple shapes in white. Introduce color, texture, or contrast with flooring, tiles, or paint. A one-off item like a Japanese-style cedar bathtub, wooden basin, or a simple bamboo mat adds organic warmth and texture. Contrasts between textures and materials, such as wood and ceramic, or concrete and glass, will enliven a potentially uniform area.

Architectural devices, like a curving dividing wall between a bathing and sleeping zone, a round shower enclosure, or an opaque glass screen, will offset clinical hard edges with sculptural forms and shadows. Simple yet inventive details like these add individuality and, if visible from outside, present a new perspective to the overall space.

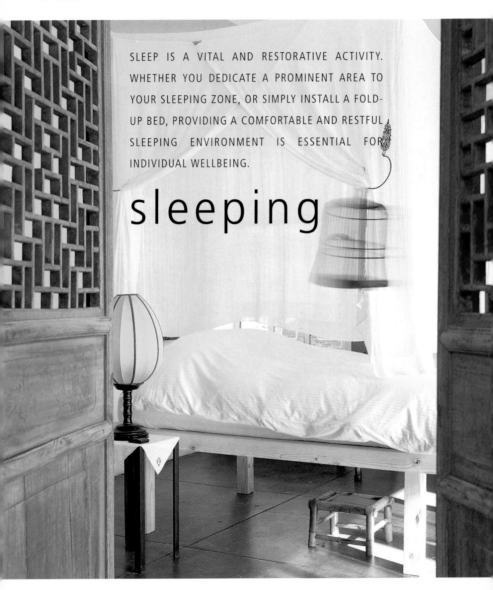

SLEEP IS A VITAL AND RESTORATIVE ACTIVITY.
WHETHER YOU DEDICATE A PROMINENT AREA TO
YOUR SLEEPING ZONE, OR SIMPLY INSTALL A FOLD-
UP BED, PROVIDING A COMFORTABLE AND RESTFUL
SLEEPING ENVIRONMENT IS ESSENTIAL FOR
INDIVIDUAL WELLBEING.

sleeping

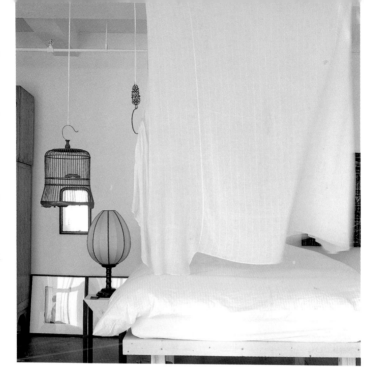

left In an expansive New York loft, oriental screens and voile drapes divide a sleeping area from the main space and provide texture and contrast to the raw industrial infrastructure.
right A voile tent transforms a simple pine bed into an intimate retreat and adds a final layer of separation within a sleep zone.

Light is a big factor when allocating an area for sleep. Depending on your personal preference, waking up to bright morning light is either an invigorating experience or an unwelcome one. If access to direct light is important to you, then position a sleeping area by a window or beneath a skylight. If morning light is not a priority, then save the good light option for another zone, perhaps cooking or relaxing.

Dedicating a zone to sleeping is a wonderful opportunity to create a retreat from the outside world and provide ideal conditions for rest. If you share your life with a partner, children, or friends, time alone is a precious event. A sleeping zone that offers a degree of separation can offer the perfect haven for a restorative or contemplative episode at any time of day.

Building a high bed base can add to a general sense of separation, while a lightweight fabric tent draped around a bed will reduce noise and, at the same time, provide a degree of privacy. Alternatively, hang fabric dividers as an effective barrier between a bed and the adjacent zone. This is a simple device that focuses attention on the bed in the sleeping zone while concealing it from

left and above
A metal sleeping platform provides an inventive sleeping area in an attic apartment. When positioning such a platform, consider the amount of space that will remain above and below.

This is a critical measurement that affects ease of use and comfort. Ideally, allow enough height above the bed for standing room on the platform. The area beneath the platform can be used as a storage space.

the rest of an open-plan environment. If space is limited, dedicating a separate area to sleeping is not always an option. Combining a sleeping zone with a different yet compatible activity is one solution, and is a good way to make the most of the available space. Alternatively, inserting a mezzanine level or sleeping platform will provide an extra level that is independent from the main space.

A mezzanine level effectively adds a new floor, or part of a new floor, to a double-height space. It is a complex structural undertaking requiring careful planning. The size and scope of a mezzanine is dependent upon the overall dimensions of your space. If extra space is essential to accommodate several individual requirements, such as a guest bedroom or a separate work area, consider inserting more than one mezzanine, or adding ones at different levels. Include independent access to each level. However, even if it is possible to insert an mezzanine, it is counterproductive to do so if one will compromise a general sense of openness and light in the interior.

Adding a small sleeping platform, just large enough for a bed, reading light, and alarm clock, is a simpler undertaking. However, although very different in size and complexity, both options offer an opportunity to introduce a new structural and visual dimension to an open-plan environment. A new level provides two-way views, both out of and into the new area, frees up space beneath, and offers a sense of separation without losing a vital connection with the main space.

Try to place a mezzanine or sleeping platform in a position where it will enjoy a special view of the interior, or has access to a window with attractive views. Bear in mind the importance of ventilation. If it is possible, insert a skylight above the new level to increase the flow of light and air, or position the new level where it will receive direct light

below The imposing dimensions of a former period sitting room provide adequate height for this space-saving solution. A compact sleeping platform fits above a kitchen area, and is accessed via a movable ladder. The platform overlooks the dining and sitting area beyond.

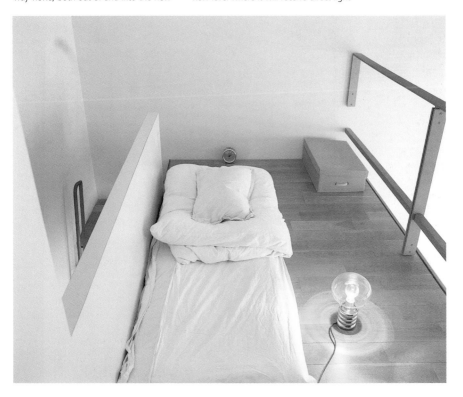

from an existing window. Nothing can compete with the good effects of waking up to natural light.

If space is at a premium, removing or moving a bed when not in use liberates a considerable amount of space and adds flexibility. A dual-function zone, perhaps combining sleeping and working, or sleeping and a child's play area, allows you to put the space to good use during the day. Mobility—perhaps a worktable on wheels, or lightweight plastic storage boxes for toys—will facilitate the crossover. Assembling and dismantling anything on a day-to-day basis is unrealistic and too time-consuming.

Fold-up beds, where the bed lifts vertically into a storage box, are clever space-saving devices that facilitate flexible sleeping arrangements. They are ideal for a small space and also offer useful back-up accommodation. The key to fold-up efficiency is a lightweight mechanism for ease of use. Beware of labor-intensive manual designs—these soon become a chore as an everyday option. One possible disadvantage of a fold-up system is finding adequate storage for bed linen when the bed is out of the way. One solution is to build in a cupboard beside or above the folding bed box. Another option is a bed on wheels that can swivel into place or out of the way as needed. This will not clear the same amount of space as a fold-up bed, but it will shift the emphasis of a zone from one specific activity to make way for an alternative.

below In a sequence of simple movements, a fold-up bed swings vertically into a cupboard. Setting shelves into the back of the recess provides extra storage for clothes and bed linen.

left and above
What appears to be a closet in fact conceals a roomy double bed. When space is at a premium, a fold-up bed is an ingenious solution. The easy gliding mechanism of a fold-up system requires minimum effort to operate, and allows you to hide the bed away when not in use. Fold-ups are ideal for dual-function areas: they free up valuable space for a different activity, allowing a sleeping area to double as a work or play zone.

new york loft space

CASE STUDY 4

LOW-KEY LOFT SPACE

In this light, white, and functional New York loft space, a textile designer combines a place to live and work with ease and efficiency. Loose cotton slipcovers on armchairs, a long sociable dining table, lively dogs, and sleeping cats, and bundles of fresh flowers project an overall sense of welcome, calm and comfort. Yet this tranquil living space is also the centre of a buzzing international textile business.

Formerly a sewing factory in New York's Tribeca district, this space is a low-tech conversion with exposed surface power conduits and low-maintenance scrub-down floors and countertops. Four south-facing windows ranged along the length of one wall provide light for the whole space. The interior retains a sense of openness and light while providing different degrees of separation for living and working. It is a triumph of simplicity and invention.

The main living area, a logical sequence of everyday activities from kitchen to dining to sitting, extends almost the full length of one side of the loft, following a line of decorative cast-iron columns. Along the opposite side of the space are the sleeping and work areas. The sleeping area is a square box just large enough for a double bed, set one step up from the main space. Completely open on one side, with views across the living and work areas to the windows beyond, it enjoys plenty of natural light. A diagonal step running the full width of the opening adds an essential extra triangle of floor space at the bottom of the bed, providing a place to step into. Simple voile curtains pull across the opening to enclose the whole area. The change in floor level and the voile screen signal a different territory, a retreat from the buzzy world beyond.

The work zone projects a very different dynamic. A floor-to-ceiling panel, studded with rectangular glass

floor plan Access from a communal stairway leads directly into the main living zone. Three cast-iron pillars run down one side of the interior, with four south-facing windows along the end wall. An internal opening between the cooking and bathing zones allows natural light to penetrate the full length of the loft.

opposite above
Aligning the work table behind a stationary divider effectively conceals office equipment. **this page** Voile curtains and a change in floor level separate the sleeping area from the main space.

insets, is set diagonally across one corner of the space to create a semi-separate work area. The divider is an ingenious solution, allowing easy access, but also providing a degree of separation. It defines the compact work area, yet at the same time promotes a sense of openness, light, and connection.

Open shelving and a folding tray table provide storage for office supplies and papers. A work table on castors sits directly behind the divider, home to the owner's computer. An inspiration board, fabric swatches, postcards, and knick-knacks adorn the space, adding color and detail. All in all, this is a compact, efficient work area, practically invisible from the living area opposite.

Developing the space is an on-going project, with the best ideas, like the sleeping platform and divider, evolving out of the owner's determination to fit all the requirements of a busy life into an imperfect space. The simplicity of the all-white aesthetic unifies any imperfections and quirky details, and adds to an overall sense of space and light.

opposite The main living space is light and white, with the kitchen, eating, and relaxing zones down one side. The work zone is set up behind a diagonal screen, which conceals it without separating it from the main space.

right Easy-access open shelving, base units, and a tile backsplash focus the kitchen zone along one wall. The long table for food preparation, eating, and working also provides a drop zone for shopping bags.

working

WHETHER YOU DESIGNATE A SEPARATE AREA FOR WORK OR COMBINE ACTIVITIES IN A MULTIFUNCTIONAL ZONE, GOOD ORGANIZATION AND PLENTY OF FLEXIBILITY WILL HAVE A BIG IMPACT ON YOUR EFFICIENCY AND ENJOYMENT.

Investing time and effort in creating an enjoyable, comfortable, and efficient working place is essential for health and wellbeing. If working and living in the same space is a permanent arrangement, it is important to acknowledge this with a commitment to finding a work space that enjoys a source of natural light and fresh air. This can be as simple as an area beside a window that you can screen off from other zones, or as expansive as an entire mezzanine level for use as a home office. The big advantage of a permanent work space is that it allows you to leave everything where it is from one day to the next without having to clear up all your things at the end of the day.

Setting up a work place in an awkward or badly lit area in an attempt to impinge as little as possible on your living space is a mistake. It may seem like a good short-term option, but will soon develop into an unhealthy long-term one. If you work from home, equipment, paperwork, and space requirements are likely

opposite A combination of hanging paper banners and a decorative folding screen effectively separate a work zone from a main living area.

above left and right Glossy plexiglass panels set on runners screen deep shelves and slide along to provide easy access to files, but conceal all when the space reverts to domestic use in the evening.

to increase, not decrease, so finding an area that can only just accommodate a working zone is impractical, as it makes no provision for future developments.

If space is at a premium, then a dual-function area will offer you greater flexibility and freedom than an entirely separate work zone. A dual-function area does require a degree of transfer from one activity to another, but this can be as simple as wheeling a work table into the center of a space. In theory, any area that is not in use during the working day is a possible option for a work zone. For example, if you can easily convert a light and open relaxing area into a place to work, this is a good option. If the conversion requires a minor compromise to an otherwise efficient arrangement, such as storing files in another area, then the benefits are greater than the inconvenience. However, if you require frequent access to the files, this level of compromise may be unworkable as an everyday arrangement.

Consider access to your work area. It is a good idea to choose somewhere out of the way of general household traffic and to devise a degree of separation from the overall space. If you share a household with children who are at home during the

far left A small desk tucked into a quiet corner may be all you need to house your laptop, pay bills, and keep up with your correspondence.
left Reduce the visual impact and officelike effect of an extensive filing system by hiding files behind sliding panels, paper screens, or simple roll-up shades.

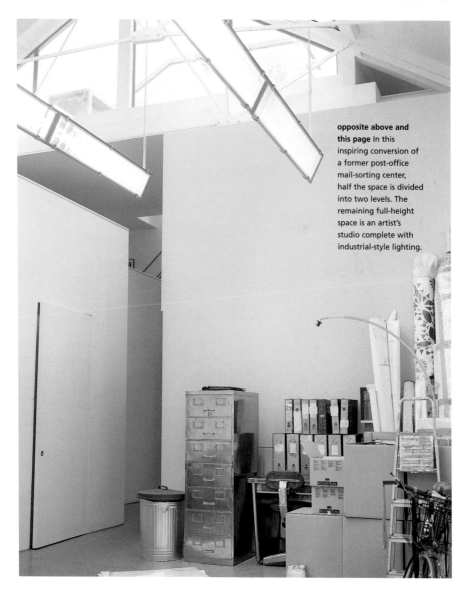

opposite above and this page In this inspiring conversion of a former post-office mail-sorting center, half the space is divided into two levels. The remaining full-height space is an artist's studio complete with industrial-style lighting.

day, taking over an area they like to use and denying them access will be problematic. If possible, work somewhere less central or popular – it will create less conflict. Alternatively, invest in mobile furniture and storage, and plan where to work on a day-to-day basis.

Good ergonomics play a key role in determining and designing an ideal work environment and are vital for health and wellbeing. If you spend several hours a day sitting down to type or draw, constantly repeating a sequence of similar movements, then it is essential to invest in a supportive, adjustable chair and an adequate table or drawing board. If you

frequently refer to a filing system, easy access is vital. Depending on the type of work you do, a kitchen table can provide a work area. However, the height of a domestic table is incompatible with an ergonomic position for typing, so this situation is not suitable for long-term keyboard use.

If you work on a computer, consider the position of the screen in relation to direct light. Avoid the glare of a back-lit screen or the mirror effect caused by direct light on a screen. As light levels change during the day, modulate them with blinds. Supplementary task lighting is an essential back-up to natural light; it is

opposite left In a compact New York apartment, an open-plan living and sleeping area undergoes a daily tranformation to a work zone for the two architect owners. **opposite right** The space is full of clever details, such as a wall of floor-to-ceiling wooden panels that slide to one side to reveal flat-folding drawing boards. **left** The wooden panels open and overlap to reveal two drawing boards that fold up from the walls. The 1950's bar stools double up as office seating.

not advisable to work long hours in an area without either. Setting up a work space in your home can require a big expenditure, especially if you need special equipment, so invest in flexible free-standing storage solutions and key items that can adapt to a review of your working habits or changes in circumstances. You can also take them with you when you move. Typical office-style furniture tends to look alien in an open-plan living space, so if you want to use this kind of furniture, it is best to screen it in some way. Traditional utilitarian metal filing cabinets and work tables look less unforgiving, but lack the slick efficiency of new products. Check out creative and ergonomic alternatives in contemporary furniture showrooms or look in architectural or design magazines for details of suppliers.

If you do not need specialized storage systems, use standard storage boxes and files. Avoid the children's playroom effect of colorful plastic bins and use metal, wood, cardboard, or clear plastic containers. Low-level storage, such as boxes under a worktable or a bench unit with a lift-up lid, is less obtrusive than high-level shelving, wall units, or cabinets. And custom-built furniture can maximize and individualize a space.

new york recycled

CASE STUDY 5

LOFT SPACE WITH A CONTAINER TRUCK

Recycling a container truck as a device to divide an open-plan interior is an extraordinary concept. Yet it provides an efficient, practical, and flexible solution. Installing it in an ex-commercial unit in midtown Manhattan imposes a powerful industrial aesthetic on a basic structural shell, unifies an irregular space, and defines and subdivides a multifunctional environment.

FLAMMABLE GAS

PULL
HERE

A photographer and theatrical set designer took on this ex-commercial unit with the intention of developing a versatile open-plan living and working environment. The challenge of a scheme like this, as with many open-plan multifunctional environments, is a complex question of how to organize the space, prioritize and integrate activities, and incorporate adequate provisions for separation. In this case, for a creative New York couple, a private sleeping area on view to visiting clients is unacceptable, whereas a large worktable hijacking much of the main living area is fine.

The space itself, a basic rectangle with an add-on square at the back, suggests a logical division into front-of-house and back-of-house activities. Positioning the everyday appliances, like the shower, kitchen sink, and stove, along a single axis also

above Using the container-truck divider to house a television and video underlines its involvement in the day-to-day activities of the loft.
right In the kitchen area, different sections of the truck siding flip up to reveal appliances and cooking preparation zones.

simplifies division and separation. For the architects, establishing this single axis became the starting point for an inventive installation in keeping with their commitment to recycling industrial cast-offs. The aluminum sides of a container truck have been installed as a divider, and effectively intersects the loft on a diagonal, drawing a dramatic and assertive line between the public and private areas.

The aluminum siding is cut into a number of different moving sections, all of which flip up, pivot, or rotate to reveal different functions. The sections look rough and heavy, yet the mechanisms that control them are precise and efficient, so lifting and opening individual sections does not require any exertion. Indeed, the ease of operation positively promotes flexibility and immediate manipulation of space.

floor plan The space is a rough rectangle with windows along one side, next to the relaxing and work areas. Two add-on squares provide a sleeping area at back and a bathing area to one side. The truck siding divides the space diagonally, extending from beside the entrance through to the bathing zone.

A wooden frame props up the aluminum siding like a billboard and supports horizontal aluminum beams running along the top and bottom of the siding. In the kitchen, two flip-up sections conceal the cooking and food preparation areas, with a cupboard door over the sink. Operating independently or together, the sections provide various combinations or degrees of openness. With all the sections shut, an abstract line-up of appliances protrudes from the aluminum. However, thanks to frequent use, all or part of the kitchen usually remains open, providing vibrant background color.

Separating the living and sleeping areas, three independent sections spin like swing doors, offering easy access and multiple variations of openness. Changing the position of the middle section also controls the angle of a built-in video and television. When the section is closed, the

television faces the main living area.
When the section is fully open, it is
possible to watch television from the bed.

The front-of-house area is a flexible
living and working area, with the
emphasis firmly on working. The main
focus of the space is one large
workstation on wheels that contains
everything relating to work. In theory the
table can be moved, but in practice it
remains in situ, the center of activity.

opposite The side of
the container truck
divides the loft
diagonally into front-
of-house working
and relaxing areas
and back-of-house
sleeping zones. The
kitchen area and
appliances are part
and parcel of the
diagonal axis itself.

above left Recycling
old commercial filing
cabinets and metal
lockers provides an
ingenious wall of
storage in the
sleeping area.
above right When
the panel containing
the television swings
round, the screen is
visible from the bed.

open-plan
essentials

dividing I lighting I storing

ONE OF THE MAIN CONCERNS OF LIVING IN AN
OPEN-PLAN HOME IS FINDING WAYS TO SUBDIVIDE
IT EFFECTIVELY. DIVIDERS ALLOW YOU TO SEPARATE
AREAS WITHOUT COMPROMISING THE OVERALL
SENSE OF SPACE AND LIGHT DISTRIBUTION.

dividing

There are many different kinds of dividers, but they roughly fall into two groups. The first group consists of permanent dividers, such as a glass-brick wall, or adjustable dividers, such as sliding panels or sections of wall. The second group is made up of freestanding dividers, such as screens, that can be moved around at will. Choose dividers that will meet your requirements in terms of space, flexibility, aesthetics, and cost efficiency.

When assessing your requirements, consider the way you use your space. Do you need to subdivide the space daily, perhaps alternating between an open-plan relaxing zone and a separate work area, or will you divide it less frequently? Will you be happy with lightweight divisions between sleeping and bathing areas, or is a more substantial partition needed? Do you require complete isolation in any part of your space – for a child's sleeping area, for example? Using dividers to change the mood of the space is another possibility, allowing you to transform an open living space into an intimate one, or introduce a new configuration of space to suit a change in season or activity.

Permanent divisions can compromise versatility, especially in more compact spaces. However, there are advantages to fixed dividers. A low-level partition wall between public and private areas, for instance, can incorporate the services and utilities for

opposite A simple wooden frame supports plexiglass panels set in a curve to divide living and sleeping areas and provide storage.
above left and center Inexpensive curtain track hung with plastic sheeting separates a sleeping area from the main living zone.
above right Simple voile drapes conceal a wall of storage in an open-plan living and bathing area, and provide a degree of separation between different zones.

below A change in
floor covering can act
as an effective divider.
Here, a change from
wood to carpeting
maps out different
zones within a loft.

a kitchen or bathing area, or provide generous storage space on
both sides of the wall. To retain a sense of openness, leave
openings on each side of a fixed partition, or a gap between the
top of the panel and the ceiling. If a floor-to-ceiling partition is
essential for insulation or privacy, use opaque glass or glass bricks
or knock through internal windows to boost light distribution
and create a sense of connection throughout the space.

If you want to install stationary dividers yet retain optimum
flexibility, opt for moving, sliding, swiveling, pivoting, or folding
panels. These will enable you to carve up a space into several
different areas without compromising versatility or provision for
privacy, allowing the interior to revert to maximum openness
when desired. Where the panels are stored when not in use, and
how easy they are to operate, are both important considerations.
When not fully extended, sliding panels usually cover a section of
wall, overlap each other, or slot away neatly into a recess in a
wall. Pivoting or folding panels usually close up and fold away
flat in a recess in a wall, like giant shutters. Both sliding and
pivoting panels require recessed metal tracks set into the floor
and ceiling to support them. Recessed tracks in the floor are not
always strictly necessary, but they do add stability. For panels that
slot into a wall recess, put retractable handles on the edge.

opposite below left This kitchen offers many levels of enclosure and division, with flip-down panels to hide work surfaces, sliding panels to shut it off, and roll-up shades. **opposite below right** Panels with retractable handles on recessed runners allow a frequent and easy reconfiguration of space.

left In a spacious New York loft, moving dividers facilitate frequent changeovers from an open-plan mezzanine to two sleeping enclosures and a bathing area. **above** A two-way opening in an opaque glass panel cleverly screens off a bathing area without blocking natural light.

Mobile screens can perform a similar function to built-in panels, but they give you the freedom to reconfigure space in any way at any time. Japanese paper and wood screens, folding wooden screens, and hospital-style fabric and metal screens all provide different degrees of separation and are appropriate to different styles of interior. Alternatively, make your own screens with plywood panels and flat hinges. Or, for a quick solution, throw fabric over a clothesrod on wheels. Large paintings, a sheet of plastic, fabric, or paper banners, strings of beads, or metal chains hanging from ceiling rods or hooks will all effectively demarcate space and will combat a lack of variation in a featureless interior.

Decoration and furnishings can also indicate a change in area or activity, effectively dividing a single space into several different zones. A change in floor covering, from concrete paving slabs to wooden floorboards, or rubber tiles to woolen carpet or rugs, can help differentiate between a hard-working public area and a relaxing private one. Arrange furniture, especially key items like sofas and tables, in social groupings to define different activity areas. And use large pieces of furniture like bookcases or cabinets to divide space. Color can also unify or divide a space. Paint a wall or use a single-color rug or a series of chairs in identical or coordinating colors to draw attention to a specific grouping or divide an open-plan scheme visually.

above left A narrow bathing area has been slotted in between sleeping and working zones and is separated from the living area by a sheet of clear glass covered with a sliding plastic panel that provides essential privacy.

opposite This sophisticated track system supports lightweight corrugated-plastic panels that divide private and public areas without blocking light in a potentially dark and gloomy semi-underground space.

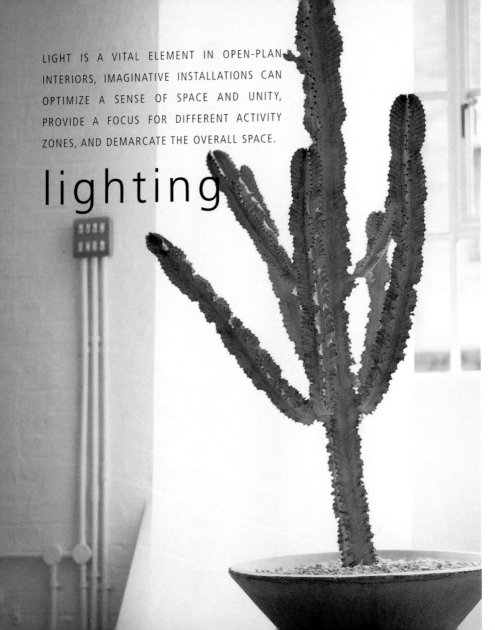

LIGHT IS A VITAL ELEMENT IN OPEN-PLAN
INTERIORS, IMAGINATIVE INSTALLATIONS CAN
OPTIMIZE A SENSE OF SPACE AND UNITY,
PROVIDE A FOCUS FOR DIFFERENT ACTIVITY
ZONES, AND DEMARCATE THE OVERALL SPACE.

lighting

Looking at the way natural light affects different parts of a space is a good starting point for deciding how to organize an open-plan environment. It makes sense to devote the best-lit areas to key zones, such as relaxing or cooking and eating. Any area with a good supply of light will always be a welcoming space.

If it is possible and cost-efficient to reconfigure your space in any way, it is worth increasing the amount of incoming light by inserting new windows or skylights or enlarging existing ones. Removing or reducing the size of internal walls, inserting internal windows or, in a space on more than one level, removing part of a floor to create a double-height opening, will all have a dramatic effect on light distribution and will enhance dark areas by providing access to natural light. White walls, ceilings, or floors and glass walls or floors, especially on mezzanine levels or galleries, will improve light levels. Shiny surfaces such as glass, metal, and plastic will also animate a space by reflecting light.

Modulating the amount of incoming light is easy. Window treatments such as roll-up shades, Venetian blinds, or curtains are all inexpensive solutions and offer privacy when needed. To diffuse light or screen an unappealing view, hang paper banners or shades at the window. If it is necessary to block out light completely, install shutters or blackout blinds.

above left Roll-up shades modulate the incoming light at expansive windows. **above center and right** Venetian blinds control light levels and can black out the space when darkness is required. **opposite** In an ex-industrial space with large metal-frame windows, a banner of tracing paper hanging from a metal pole diffuses light and adds an element of privacy.

Use artifical light to supplement natural light and to add versatility and variation to a space. Artificial lighting falls into four groups: ambient, task, accent, and information. Ambient lighting is general background lighting that throws light over a wide area. Task lighting illuminates one area to aid a specific task or activity. Accent lighting can highlight an architectural feature or decorative object. Information lighting helps you move around a space safely, illuminating a change in floor-level, for example. A combination of all four types will create a comfortable, user-friendly environment.

Different light sources and fixtures create different effects. Halogen lighting is cool and modern, while tungsten is warm and mellow. Fluorescent lighting can create similar effects to both halogen and tungsten, and has the added bonus of being ecologically friendly. There is an enormous choice of different fixtures available. The ones you choose will depend on personal preference, but it is important to make sure the fixtures will do exactly what you want them to. Central ceiling lights create a pool of light and can indicate a key area, such as a relaxing zone. Add other lights, such as floor and table lamps, to enliven the scheme. Spotlights throw a strong pool of light and can usually be adjusted to suit different uses and activities. Track and barewire lighting carry miniature spotlights, which can be individually

opposite below left In a workshop conversion in Paris, a decorative central light adorns a simple eating area.
opposite below center This versatile aluminum fixture can be used as a spotlight or an uplighter.
opposite below right Minimalist in feel, track and barewire lighting offers a flexible alternative to fixed spotlights.

below Adjustable shiny chrome wall lights are used here as uplighters to bounce light off a white ceiling and illuminate a small reading area.
right Recycling a hospital light as a task light in this kitchen area is in keeping with the large scale of the space, the industrial feel and the owner's heavy-duty catering equipment.

opposite A mix of fluorescent tube lighting concealed behind sliding plastic panels and a sculptural Tom Dixon floor light animate and add color to a pared-down interior.

right Decorative floor lights provide illumination but also bring interest and atmosphere to an interior.

below A simple detail like matching lights and paint shades transforms three simple wall recesses into a focal point in a low-key relaxation zone.

angled or adjusted, on tensioned cables. Uplighters and downlighters reflect light in a particular direction. Uplighters bounce light off the walls and ceiling, and provide soft, diffused, illumination, while downlighters cast a pool of light downward, like a spotlight. There are many types of uplighter on the market, while downlighters are often recessed in the ceiling.

The arrangement and combination of different types of lighting can unify or divide a space just as effectively as any structural dividers by creating different effects, illuminating an overall space, or focusing on a specific area. In a multifunctional area such as a relaxing zone, install ambient lights with dimmers and provide selective accent or decorative lighting for contrast. Use task lighting to signal areas set aside for activities such as reading or working on the computer. In a kitchen or work area, it is essential to provide adequate task lighting.

Installing new lighting can be disruptive, so wiring in fixtures, sockets, and switches should take place in conjunction with any other building work. Calculate how many electrical sockets and light fixtures you require for different activities or zones. In a space with a large floor area, install sockets in the floor for maximum flexibility. A qualified electrician will be able to give you advice, assess your electrical infrastructure, and let you know if your current system needs updating or extending.

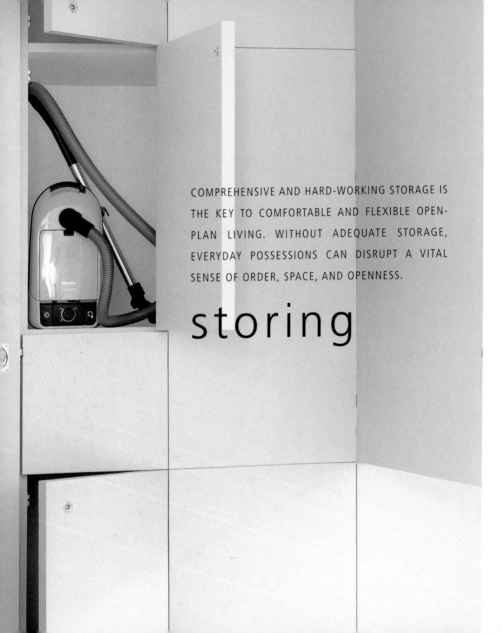

COMPREHENSIVE AND HARD-WORKING STORAGE IS THE KEY TO COMFORTABLE AND FLEXIBLE OPEN-PLAN LIVING. WITHOUT ADEQUATE STORAGE, EVERYDAY POSSESSIONS CAN DISRUPT A VITAL SENSE OF ORDER, SPACE, AND OPENNESS.

storing

opposite A large square "pod" in the center of an open-plan interior contains bathing and sleeping areas as well as ample storage space.

Providing adequate provision for storage is the key to organizing an open-plan environment. Storage solutions can resolve basic issues such as where to keep clothing and kitchen items, or conceal bulky pieces of equipment such as televisions, washing machines, and computers. In a multifunctional environment, good storage will help you to retain flexibility, visual simplicity, and freedom of choice.

It is often more practical to devote a substantial proportion of space to storage to ease pressure on a general living space, rather than maintain maximum space at the expense of comfort and practicality. In Japanese homes, where space is a critical issue, one-third of every household is taken up by storage. Although this may seem like a disproportionate amount of storage to living space, adequate storage can make an open-plan home more flexible, allowing for simple and efficient changeovers between different activities, such as relaxing or working or sleeping.

Be realistic about storage requirements in an open-plan interior. Creating a sense of space and order is

above This low-level storage unit offers a variety of open cubes, shelving, and drawers. Units like this look unobtrusive and orderly, and accommodate large amounts of essential equipment.

left Rows of identical cardboard boxes neatly stacked in a basic industrial-style shelving system provide an easily accessible home for papers, photos, and out-of-season clothes.

not always about finding a home for every single possession, but about living with what is essential and functional. Edit your possessions and select a capsule collection of kitchenware, entertainment equipment, clothing, and other key items, then design and plan your storage solutions accordingly.

The basic options for different kinds of storage are either structural systems, such as a dividing wall with built-in shelves or cupboards, stationary systems, such as wall-mounted shelving or modular units, or freestanding storage. All of these options can provide open storage for display or conceal items in some way.

Many contemporary architects incorporate built-in storage in structural features, using perimeter or dividing walls to conceal streamlined floor-to-ceiling cupboards that can accommodate the essential clutter of everyday life. Built-in storage can also make use of irregular structural details or otherwise unused space in a way that ready-made storage items cannot, by tucking a custom-made clothes rod or drawer unit beneath a sloping ceiling, for example, or fitting drawers into stair treads. Stationary storage, such as wall-mounted modular systems, presents plenty of functional options for both concealed storage and display space. Freestanding and mobile storage is highly flexible, as it can be moved around from area to area as needed.

Different areas require different storage provisions. In a kitchen area, the emphasis is on quick and easy access to key items. Store utensils that are in frequent use within an arm's length of the work area. Ideally, keep pots and pans next to the

above right Sliding plastic panels conceal a compact wedge-shaped storage area, which extends the full length of an small open-plan apartment

right Chunky open shelves set in front of a window create a focal point in a long, narrow kitchen area. The shelves provide storage space, but do not block light.

left In a compact space, clever details, like this sleek streamlined metal holder for a roll of paper towels, make the most of the available space. **below left** This precise made-to-measure storage unit has been squeezed into a tiny gap in a small kitchen zone. It brings a bright splash of color to the kitchen area, and makes use of what would otherwise be wasted space.

below Functional laboratory-style units, a stainless steel backsplash, and suspended glass shelving optimize the available space in a New York kitchen with an industrial aesthetic.

oven or cooktop, fresh vegetables adjacent to the food-preparation area, and kitchenware in close proximity to the dishwasher for easy unloading. When planning storage for a kitchen area, bear in mind that whatever you install is likely to be visible from the main living area, if not from every part of the space, so flexible dividers such as flip-up or sliding panels or shades that pull down to screen the kitchen area will allow you to conceal clutter. Choose a combination of freestanding items and open shelving or built-in wall and base units, depending on your requirements. Low-level mobile storage units are space-efficient additions to any kitchen area and can be stored under work surfaces and wheeled out when they are needed.

A flexible storage system is essential in a multifunctioning living space, especially if you live as a family or with several other people. Leaving all your possessions in full view can look cluttered and untidy, yet if everything is hidden away an area can look sterile and anonymous. Aim to reveal a few items that represent different activities, but conceal large CD or book collections. Sliding panels, roll-up shades, or mobile screens can hide electrical equipment or a wall of books, yet still allow easy access to the items. In a living area, storage options include wall-mounted units, low-level shelving or cabinets, freestanding cupboards, or modular cube systems. A mobile computer desk for your laptop or an entertainment system on a wheeled trolley is a flexible storage option, as it can be pushed out into a central position when needed, then stashed away in a different area afterward.

As well as storage items designed for the domestic market, there are many alternatives available from commercial or trade suppliers, such as catering, retail, office, and medical storage systems. The large scale and utilitarian design of these products means that they fit in well with ex-industrial interiors. And on a practical level, items originally made to industrial or commercial standards provide greater storage capacity than their domestic counterparts. However, a filing cabinet or airline locker takes up lots of space, so avoid overwhelming a compact scheme with over-sized furniture.

opposite left A glossy red trolley with drawers acts as a mobile storage center for CDs, DVDs, a telephone, and directories.
opposite center Using secondhand catering equipment for storage is in keeping with the scale and industrial aesthetic of this kitchen area.
opposite right A versatile folding trolley stores flat when not in use and provides an extra work surface in the kitchen area at a moment's notice.

above left This inventive custom-made storage system utilizes the wasted space beneath stair treads by using them as a chest of drawers.
above center A metal bucket hanging from a rope and pulley can be lowered to give access to household items or raised so it is out of view.
above right Clever design maximizes the potential of this mini closet. It contains a small fold-down ironing board and pull-out clothes rod.

a practical
approach

heating I insulation I ventilation I noise I assessing change

Creating an ideal living environment is a matter of individual taste, although fresh air and warmth are vital for everyone's wellbeing. And while simple joys like opening a window on a spring morning or lighting a stove in winter are rewarding emotional and physical pleasures, even the most elemental domestic space will benefit from some degree of ventilation and heating.

In an open-plan home, devising effective service systems requires precise planning and assessment. As a general guide, when choosing new service systems or upgrading, adapting, or extending existing ones, consider all aspects of performance, the cost of installation, and level of disruption, running costs, aesthetics, flexibility, and maintenance.

Many conventional domestic systems work well in open-plan apartments and conversions built to standard proportions. Yet the proportions and expansiveness of some conversions, especially former non-domestic spaces like schools or light-industrial factories, often require a combination of high performance products and systems.

Heating In general, domestic heating is usually supplied via convenient, cost-effective central heating systems or by a series of independent heaters.

Central heating systems are either wet or dry systems. Wet systems heat water in a boiler using gas, electricity, solid fuel, wood, or oil, and distribute the hot water via pipes to radiators, convector radiators, and underfloor heating pipes. Individual thermostats can adjust the temperature on different radiators and floor and wall convector radiators, whereas a single thermostat sets the temperature for all trench convector radiators and underfloor heating pipes. Wet systems usually heat the domestic hot water supply, too.

Dry systems use gas, electricity, or oil-fueled heaters to warm air and distribute it through a system of ducts, grilles, and convector heaters. A central thermostat controls air temperature throughout the system. However, with an additional cooling coil, dry systems can distribute cold air as well as hot, which is a big bonus in hot weather. Heating ducts transmit sound as well as air, so avoid placing machines or equipment next to vents or outlets. Both wet and dry heating systems take moisture out of the air, so it is essential to keep fresh air circulating. Humidifiers and dehumidifiers can adjust air-moisture content. Alternatively, a simple bowl of water on the floor, Japanese-style, will restore moisture to dry air—drop in a pebble for visual interest.

Radiators, exclusive to wet systems, are available in every size, style, and color imaginable, and can be anchored to walls or stand on floors. They are usually made from steel, although cast iron and aluminum models are also available. Different configurations of coils and fins deliver different amounts of heat, so calculate performance in conjunction with aesthetics.

Radiators are efficient, economical, easy to control, and require little maintenance.

Bear in mind that if you have an expansive open-plan environment with radiators attached to the perimeter walls, heat can take some time to radiate to the center of the space. An electric ceiling fan, or series of fans, can help circulation Alternatively, you could find a way of fixing a radiator (or radiators) in the center of the space—perhaps using an existing architectural feature like a column. Incorporating an additional heating source, such as a stove or underfloor heating system will also prevent potential cold spots.

Good air circulation around each radiator ensures maximum heat radiation, so try not to restrict air flow with big items of furniture like sofas or bookcases. Depending on the available wall space, this may present a problem. Radiators often occupy premium wall space, which can leave big pieces of furniture and paintings with no place to go. Work out a floor plan before installation to avoid any conflicts. Finally, resist the temptation to use radiators for drying wet clothes, as this will create a build-up of condensation.

Convector radiators blow hot or cold air and run on electricity or are connected to either wet or dry heating systems. Compact and unobtrusive, with grill fascias, they can be mounted on walls or ceilings or, ideally, set in trenches in flooring, beneath cabinets, or in stair treads and baseboards. For visual simplicity and to reduce the dust-trap effect of grill fascias, install convector radiators in a recess or box and conceal them with metal or wooden ventilation panels that are in keeping with the architectural style of the space.

opposite above right Vertical radiators are highly visible, so stick to simple colors and designs. Fitting them in a recess or niche makes them less obtrusive.

above left These basic, low-budget radiators are low-key and unobtrusive.

above center If you have the space, original cast-iron radiators provide substantial levels of heat. Sand-blast to remove paint and seal them to keep them free from rust.

above right A trench radiator with metal grille delivers heat all along a line of sliding plastic panels that separate living and sleeping areas.

top and above
Fresh air is vital.
Make sure all your
windows open and
consider installing
a ventilation system
to boost air
circulation. Always
install extractors in
cooking areas.

Underfloor heating pipes, unlike convector heaters in trenches, will heat up an entire floor. This is invisible heating with a high comfort factor. Most underfloor heating pipes run off wet systems, circulating hot water through thermoplastic pipes set in concrete or an underfloor cavity. Installation involves pulling up the whole floor, so this option is a big commitment, a big effort and a big expense. However, the water circulating through the system is not as hot as the water that circulates in a wet radiator system, so underfloor heating is cost-efficient to use. And if run in combination with a radiator system, it is possible to recycle some of the warm water. All-round good insulation is essential to minimize heat loss.

Stoves that run on gas, wood, or solid fuel generate a great deal of heat and provide a striking focal point in an interior. They are capable of running a central heating system, but are most commonly used to heat hot water and boost central heating systems. Stoves are high maintenance, requiring regular cleaning and fresh fuel every few hours (except gas stoves), so are more labor intensive on a day-to-day basis. Strict safety precautions apply for flue maintenance and installation, and it is advisable to check with your local authority about any fuel restrictions.

Other forms of heating worth considering include solar systems, which are ecologically friendly, simple to install,

require a good supply of sunshine, access to a roof to install solar panels or sheets, and a back-up system for when sunshine is not on the menu. Freestanding electric storage heaters provide low-cost background heating in a big space, but they take up a lot of room. Electric fans, electric element heaters, or gas storage-bottle heaters are all adequate sources of additional localized heat.

Insulation Generating heat is only one part of the equation—reducing your heat loss and fuel consumption is just as important. Practical insulating measures like attaching draft excluders to doors and windows as well as insulating roof space, pipes, and hot water tanks will all significantly reduce heat loss. Professional measures like insulating cavity walls, floors, and ceilings, and double-glazing windows will also maximize efficiency. However, it takes a little time to see a return on your investment in terms of savings on your fuel bills. If you are planning a total refit of your home, or other major building work, incorporating these measures at the same time will be less disruptive and less expensive.

Ventilation Good ventilation is essential to prevent a build-up of moisture and condensation, which creates an unhealthy living environment and can damage the fabric of a building. Opening windows is the simplest way to keep fresh air circulating. You could also install ceiling fans in large spaces or areas away from open windows to ensure an air current. Install ventilation fans to expel stale air and draw in fresh air. In compliance with standard public health and safety regulations, install extractor fans in cooking and bathing areas—they will remove excessive moisture and potential condensation and eliminate smells to maintain a healthy, pleasant atmosphere.

Noise One inevitable effect of introducing effective heating and ventilation systems is a general increase in ambient noise levels. Incorporating good insulation in the fabric of the building will significantly reduce the amount of noise entering from outside, while insulating pipes, boilers, cisterns, and ducts, including at points of entry and exit, should also significantly reduce amounts of internal noise.

Wherever possible, isolate and insulate domestic machines such as tumble dryers and washing machines in a purpose-built utility cupboard or alcove. Other possible solutions are a combination, or possibly compromise, of planning and design decisions and individual aesthetics. For example, in simple architectural interiors with bare floors and walls, sound will echo and multiply in ratio to the number of people in the space. Using thick, sound-absorbing rugs to define different areas of activity and hanging fabric shades will help to alleviate the echo problem and cut down on noise transference. However, a degree of ambient noise and noise transference is, unfortunately, a factor of one-space living.

Assessing change Reducing heat loss, fuel consumption, and noise pollution and maintaining a clean and healthy living environment are all ecologically friendly objectives. Deficient, outdated services are inefficient and uneconomical, so it seems a logical step to replace them with more up-to-date efficient systems. Whatever level of change or installation you envisage, get professional advice to assess what already exists, what is possible, and what products and systems are relevant to your requirements. Even simple projects like upgrading the existing radiators on a wet system may require an upgrade in your boiler as well. Likewise with electricity—it is essential to check electrical systems are safe and capable of supporting everyday requirements. New appliances may require new circuitry.

As a general rule, the simpler the layout of a system, the fewer the potential problems. Keep a plan of piping, ducts, and wiring to assist with maintenance and servicing. Quick access to stopcocks and circuit breakers is essential in an emergency—ideally, install them in an area with easy access, like an understairs cupboard or behind a panel in the wall or floor, and clearly label all pipes, switches, and stopcocks in view.

suppliers

STRUCTURAL SOLUTIONS

American Institute of Architects
www.aia.org
The AIA website provides helpful information on what an architect can do for you, plus tips on working with an architect. Use their architect finder service to find an AIA member near you.

National Construction Estimator
www.get-a-quote.net
Labor and material cost estimates for residential, commercial, or industrial construction projects.

Your Complete Home
www.yourcompletehome.com
Provides listings for contractors in every state, as well as helpful information about financing, hiring, and do-it-yourself projects.

KITCHENS

DuPont Corian®
800 426 7426
www.dupont.com/corian
Nonporous acrylic surface for counters and sinks. Stains or scratches can be ground out.

IKEA
Visit www.ikea.com to find your nearest store.
Stylish, affordable cabinet designs. Also inexpensive storage, lighting, and other home accessories.

KitchenBath.com
738 Franklin Avenue, Suite B
Franklin Square, NY 11010
800 646 1305
www.lasalesco.com
Mini kitchens including compact kitchenettes incorporating refrigerator, cooktop, and sink; tabletop dishwashers and compact washer/driers.

Poggenpohl
Visit www.poggenpohl-usa.com to find your nearest showroom or dealer.
European kitchen design with clean modern lines.

BATHROOMS

American Standard
Call 800 359 3261or visit www.americanstandard-us.com for details of your nearest stockist.
Wall-mounted basins and other sanitaryware.

Butler Manufacturing Company
1540 Genessee
Kansas City MO 64102
816 968 3000
www.butlermfg.com
Manufacturers of "intelligent" electro-polarizing glass.

Kohler Co.
Call 800 456-4537 or visit www.kohlerco.com to find a retailer near you.
Modern bathroom and kitchen furniture, plumbing, and sinks.

Priva-lite
www.sggprivalite.com
Revolutionary glass that can be switched from clear to translucent, ensuring optimal vision control.

Tile Mosaics.com
8133 Firestone Boulevard
Downey CA 90241
562 904 8446
www.tilemosaics.com
Supplier of mosaic tiles.

DIVIDERS

Acme Brick Co.
800 932 2263
www.brick.com
Glass-block walls.

Avanti Systems
877 282 6843
www.avantisystemsusa.com
Innovative design-led partition and wall solutions, including sliding glass doors and walls.

Chopa Imports
800 961-2555
www.chopa.com
Japanese-style rice paper screens and doors.

The Folding Sliding Door Company
702 385 2447
www.foldingslidingdoors.us
Design, manufacture, and install aluminum or wood folding sliding doors.

Kalwall
800 258 9777
www.kalwall.com
A translucent building panel that extracts and converts energy from the sun to heat, cool, and naturally light buildings. Can be used for walls, windows, and skylights
.

Kolbe & Kolbe
1323 S 11th Avenue
Wausau, WI 54401
Call 800 955 8177 or visit www.kolbe-kolbe.com to find a retailer near you.
Windows and internal and external doors.

Smith & Noble
800 248 8888
www.smithandnoble.com
Vertical and horizontal shades, Roman shades, and cornice boxes in all materials.

Wausau Window & Wall
1415 West Street
Wausau, WI 54401
715 845 2161 or
877 678 2983
www.wausauwindows.com
Custommade windows and curtain walls, sliding doors, and horizontal sliders.

STORAGE

California Closets
Call 888 336 9797 or visit www.calclosets.com to find a retailer near you.
Custom-built closets.

Hold Everything

Call 212 879 1450 or visit
www.holdeverything.com to
find your nearest store.
*Everything for storage, from
baskets to shelves to clothes
hangers.*

Poliform

Call 888 765 4367 for a
catalog or visit
www.poliformusa.com to find
a retailer near you.
*Chic Italian closet and
bookcase design specialists.*

LIGHTING

International Association of Lighting Designers

Merchandise Mart
Suite 487
200 World Trade Center
Chicago, IL 60654
312 527 3677
www.iald.org
*Offers a useful referral service
that can provide the names of
lighting designers working in
your area.*

Kichler Lighting Group

800 659 9000 or
216 573 1000
www.kichler.com
*Any type of lighting,including
under-counter fluorescents.*

The Lighting Center Ltd

240 East 59th Street
New York, NY 10022
212 888 8388
www.lightingcenter-ny.com
*Distributors of literally
hundreds of different
European and American
lighting collections.*

Lightolier

Call 508 679 8131 or visit
www.lightolier.com for details
of your nearest store.
*All types of contemporary
lighting, both practical and
decorative.*

WAC Lighting

113–125 14th Avenue
College Point, NY 11356
800 526 2588
www.waclighting.com
*Manufacturers of discreet
track and recessed lighting.*

FLOORING

Advance Terrazzo Inc.

1217 East Gibson Lane
Phoenix, AZ 85034
800 323 9736 or
602 253 9400
www.advanceterrazzo.com
*With over 50 marble, glass,
and plastic aggregates, they
can match any paint coloring
when laying chips in resin
flooring, or create specific
mosaic designs.*

Anderson Hardwood Flooring

Visit www.andersonfloors.com
to find a retailer near you.
Durable hardwood flooring.

Classic Tile Inc.

325 Pine Street
Elizabeth, NJ 07206
908 289 8400
www.classictile.com
*Installers and distributors of
Estrie and Flexco textured
rubber flooring, as well as
Congoleum, Formica,
Wicander vinyl-clad cork,
poured rubber floors, and
many other quality resilient
flooring surfaces.*

FURNITURE

ABC Carpet & Home

888 Broadway
New York, NY 10003
212 473 3000
Visit www.ABC.com for
details of your nearest store.
*An eclectic collection of
furnishings, linens, rugs, and
accessories.*

B & B Italia USA

150 East 58th Street
New York, NY 10155
800 872 1697
www.bebitalia.it
*Cutting-edge Italian designer
furniture by Bellini, Cittero,
Pesce, Scarpa, and other
notable designers.*

Chiasso

www.chiasso.com
*Chic, streamlined modern
furniture, accessories, rugs,
and textiles.*

The Conran Shop

Bridgemarket
407 East 59th Street
New York, NY 10022
Call 866 755 9079 for a
catalog
www.conran.com
*Simply designed and stylish
modern furniture, lighting,
glassware, kitchenware, and
decorative accents.*

Crate & Barrel

646 N. Michigan Avenue
Chicago, IL 60611
Call 800 996 9960 or visit
www.crateandbarrel.com to
find your nearest store.
*Good-value furniture and
accessories.*

Create-A-Bed

1 877 966 3852
www.wallbed.com
*Murphy wall beds to put
together yourself.*

Design Within Reach

Visit www.dwr.com to find
your nearest store.
*Modern designer classics to
buy online, including
furniture, storage, accessories,
and textiles.*

Highbrow Inc.

2110 8th Avenue South
Nashville, TN 37204
888 329 0219
www.highbrowfurniture.com
*Dealer of vintage modern
furniture, textiles, and
lighting.*

Jensen-Lewis

89 Seventh Avenue
New York, NY 10011
212 929 4880
www.jensen-lewis.com
*Well-priced modern furniture
and accessories.*

Modlivin

5327 East Colfax Avenue
Denver, CO 80220
720 941 9292
www.modlivin.com
*A good selection of mid-
century modern furniture and
accessories.*

Murphy Beds Direct

888 730 3003
www.murphybedsdirect.com
*Murphy wall beds in different
sizes and styles.*

business credits

ARCHITECTS AND DESIGNERS WHOSE WORK IS FEATURED IN THIS BOOK

Babylon Design Ltd
301 Fulham Road
London SW10 9QH
+44 20 7376 7233
www.babylonlondon.com
Pages 14, 23, 100–101, 125 right

Claire Bataille & Paul ibens
Vekestraat 13 Bus 14
2000 Antwerpen, Belgium
+32 3 213 86 20
www.bataille-ibens.be
Pages 1 center, 3, 18, 40–45, 121 left, 129 top left

Briffa Phillips
19–21 Holywell Hill
St Albans, Herts AL1 1EZ
+44 1727 840 567
www.briffaphillips.com
Pages 26 top, 26–27, 62–63, 82, 83 top left and below left

Brookes Stacey Randall
For this project :
Space Craft Architects
16 Winchester Walk
London SE1 9AQ

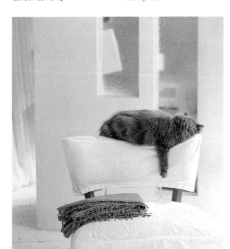

+44 20 7407 9394
www.spacecraft-architects.com
Pages 1 right, 32-33, 68-69, 112–113, 116 below both, 117 right, 127 top

dMFK (de Metz Forbes Knight Architects), formerly de Metz Architects
Unit 4, 250 Finchley Road
London NW3 6DN
+44 20 7435 1144
www.dmfk.co.uk
Pages 15 left and right, 92 all, 130 right

Jamie Falla/MooArc
198 Blackstock Road
London N5 1EN
+44 20 7354 1729
www.mooarc.com
Pages 25 below, 48 and 49 left, 66-67, 87 both

Han Feng
Fashion designer
333 West 39th Street, 12th floor
New York, NY 10018
212 695 9509
www.hanfeng.com
Pages 16, 31 right, 50–51, 84–85, 88–89, 115 top right, 136 top left

Fernlund and Logan Architects
414 Broadway
New York, NY 10013
212 925 9628
www.fernlundlogan.com
Pages 7 right, 12–13, 46–47, 54–55, 116–117 center, 135 left

Alastair Hendy
Food writer, art director and designer
www.alastairhendy.com
Pages 4, 10–11, 34 left, 72–79, 102 below right, 120, 123 right, 125 left, 130 center, 131 left, 135 center, 136 below left, 144 center

**Brian Johnson
Johnson Naylor**
+44 20 7490 8885
www.johnsonnaylor.co.uk
Pages 2, 26 below, 56–61, 122 center, 134, 144 right

Steven Learner Studio
307 Seventh Avenue
Room 2201
New York, NY 10001
212 741 8583
www.stevenlearnerstudio.com
Pages 52–53, 80–81, 116 top left, 123 left

Littman Goddard Hogarth
61 Courtfield Gardens
London SW5 0NQ
+44 20 7565 8366
www.hogartharchitects.co.uk
Pages 71, 86 all, 93, 102 below left, 126, 128 below, 129 below left, 144 left

LOT/EK Architecture
55 Little West 12th Street
New York, NY 10014
212 255 9326
www.lot-ek.com
Pages 28, 29 left, 106–111

Marino + Giolito
161 West 16th Street
New York, NY 10011
212 675 5737
marino.giolito@rcn.com
Pages 104–105, 129 right

Orefelt Associates
43 Pall Mall Deposit
124–128 Barlby Road
London W10 6BL
+44 20 8960 2560
Pages 6, 24, 34 right, 102 top right, 103,

Architeam Ltd
Campfield House
Powdermill Lane
Battle
East Sussex TN33 0SY
+44 1424 775211
www.architeam.co.uk
Pages 25 top right, 35, 64 right, 65 all, 121 center and right, 122 right, 131 center

Evelyn Roussel
+33 1 43 55 76 97
Pages 20–21, 118–119, 135 right

Stickland Coombe Architecture
258 Lavender Hill
London SW11 1LJ
+44 20 7924 1699
Endpapers, pages 8–9, 124, 128 top, 130 left

Totem Design Group
71 Franklin Street
New York, NY 10013
212 925 5506
Fax: 212 925 5082
www.totemdesign.com
Pages 22, 114–115 main and top left and center

Urban Salon Ltd
Unit D, Flat Iron Yard
Ayres Street
London SE1 1ES
+44 20 7357 8800
www.urbansalonarchitects.com
Pages 70 both, 131 right

Woolf Architects
27 Swinton Street
London WC1X 9NW
+44 20 7692 1086
Pages 5,19, 30, 30–31 center, 64 top left and below left, 90 below right, 91, 132–133

picture credits

Key: t = top, b = below, l = left, r = right, c = center

1 l Gabriele Sanders' apartment in New York; 1 c an apartment in Knokke, Belgium designed by Claire Bataille and Paul ibens; 1 r Nik Randall, Suzsi Corio, and Louis' home in London designed by Brookes Stacey Randall; 2 Brian Johnson's apartment in London designed by Johnson Naylor; 3 an apartment in Knokke, Belgium designed by Claire Bataille and Paul ibens; 4 Alastair Hendy & John Clinch's apartment in London designed by Alastair Hendy; 5 Patricia Ijaz's house in London designed by Jonathan Woolf of Woolf Architects; 6 a house in London designed by Brookes Associates. Design team Gunnar Orefelt and Knut Hovland; 7 l Nik Randall, Suzsi Corio, and Louis' home in London designed by Brookes Stacey Randall; 7 r Jeff Priess and Rebecca Quaytman's apartment in New York designed by Fernlund and Logan Architects, painting by Rebecca Quaytman; 8–9 Anthony Swanson's apartment in London designed by Stickland Coombe Architecture; 10–11 Alastair Hendy & John Clinch's apartment in London designed by Alastair Hendy; 12–13 Jeff Priess and Rebecca Quaytman's apartment in New York designed by Fernlund and Logan Architects; 14 Babylon Design Studio in London Ltd.; 15 Nicki De Metz's flat in London designed by De Metz architects; 16 Han Feng's apartment in New York designed by Han Feng; 17 Christian Baquiast's apartment in Paris; 18 an apartment in Knokke, Belgium designed by Claire Bataille and Paul ibens; 19 Patricia Ijaz's house in London designed by Jonathan Woolf; 20–21 Evelyne Rousell's apartment in Paris; 22 David Shearer and Gail Schultz's apartment in New York; 23 Babylon Design Ltd. studio in London; 24 a house in London designed by Orefelt Associates, Design team Gunnar Orefelt and Knut Hovland; 25 t Andrew Noble's apartment in London designed by Nico Rensch Architeam; 25 b Jamie Falla and Lynn Graham's house in London; 26 t an apartment in Bath designed by Briffa Phillips Architects; 26 b Brian Johnson's apartment in London designed by

Johnson Naylor; 26–27 an apartment in Bath designed by Briffa Phillips Architects; 28 & 29 l Jones Miller studio in New York designed by Giuseppe Lignano and Ada Tolla of LOT/EK Architecture; 29 r Christian Baquiast's apartment in Paris; 30 l & 30–31 c Patricia Ijaz's house in London designed by Jonathan Woolf; 31 r Han Feng's apartment in New York designed by Han Feng; 32–33 Nik Randall, Suzsi Corio, and Louis' home in London designed by Brookes Stacey Randall; 34 l Alastair Hendy & John Clinch's apartment in London designed by Alastair Hendy; 34 r a house in London designed by Orefelt Associates, Design team Gunnar Orefelt and Knut Hovland; 35 Andrew Noble's apartment in London designed by Nico Rensch Architeam; 36–37 Gabriele Sanders' apartment in New York; 38 Christian Baquiast's apartment in Paris; 39 Christian Baquiast's apartment in Paris; 41–45 an apartment in Knokke, Belgium designed by Claire Bataille and Paul ibens; 46–47 Jeff Priess and Rebecca Quaytman's apartment in New York designed by Fernlund and Logan Architects; 48 & 49 l Jamie Falla and Lynn Graham's house in London; 50–51 Han Feng's apartment in New York designed by Han Feng; 52–53 the loft of Peggy and Steven Learner designed by Steven Learner Studio; 54–55 Jeff Priess and Rebecca Quaytman's apartment in New York designed by Fernlund and Logan Architects; 56–61 Brian Johnson's apartment in London designed by Johnson Naylor; 62–63 an apartment in Bath designed by Briffa Phillips Architects; 64 tl & bl Patricia Ijaz's house in London designed by Jonathan Woolf of Woolf Architects; 64 r & 65 Andrew Noble's apartment in London designed by Nico Rensch Architeam; 66–67 Jamie Falla and Lynn Graham's house in London; 68–69 Nik Randall, Suzsi Corio, and Louis' home in London designed by Brookes Stacey Randall; 70 both Lucy Guard's apartment in London designed by Urban Salon; 71 an apartment in London designed by Littman Goddard Hogarth Architects; 72–79 Alastair Hendy & John Clinch's apartment in London designed by Alastair Hendy; 80–81 the loft of Peggy and Steven Learner designed by Steven Learner Studio; 82-83 an

apartment in Bath designed by Briffa Phillips Architects; 84–85 Han Feng's apartment in New York designed by Han Feng; 86 an apartment in London designed by Littman Goddard Hogarth Architects; 87 Jamie Falla and Lynn Graham's house in London; 88–89 Han Feng's apartment in New York designed by Han Feng; 90 tl & tr Christian Baquiast's apartment in Paris; 90 br & 91 Patricia Ijaz's house in London designed by Jonathan Woolf of Woolf Architects; 92 Nicki De Metz's flat in London designed by De Metz architects; 93 an apartment in London designed by Littman Goddard Hogarth Architects; 94–99 Gabriele Sanders' apartment in New York, 99 chairs from Totem; 100–101 Babylon Design Ltd. studio in London; 102 bl an apartment in London designed by Littman Goddard Hogarth Architects; 102br Alastair Hendy & John Clinch's apartment in London designed by Alastair Hendy; 102 tr & 103 a house in London designed by Orefelt Associates, Design team Gunnar Orefelt and Knut Hovland; 104–105 Chelsea Studio New York City, designed by Marino and Giolito; 106–111 Jones Miller studio in New York designed by Giuseppe Lignano and Ada Tolla of LOT/EK Architecture; 112–113 Nik Randall, Suzsi Corio, and Louis' home in London designed by Brookes Stacey Randall; 114 & inset & 115 c David Shearer and Gail Schultz's apartment in New York; 115 tr Han Feng's apartment in New York designed by Han Feng; 115 tl the loft of Peggy and Steven Learner designed Steven Learner Studio; 116 b both Nik Randall, Suzsi Corio, and Louis' home in London designed by Brookes Stacey Randall; 116–117 c Jeff Priess and Rebecca Quaytman's apartment in New York designed by Fernlund and Logan Architects; 117 r Nik Randall, Suzsi Corio, and Louis' home in London designed by Brookes Stacey Randall; 118–119 Evelyn Rousell's apartment in Paris; 120 Alastair Hendy & John Clinch's apartment in London designed by Alastair Hendy; 121 l an apartment in Knokke, Belgium designed by Claire Bataille and Paul ibens; 121 c & r Andrew Noble's apartment in London designed by Nico Rensch Architeam; 122 l Nello Renault's loft in Paris; 122 c Brian Johnson's apartment in London designed by Johnson Naylor; 122 r Andrew Noble's apartment in London designed by Nico Rensch

Architeam; 123 l the loft of Peggy and Steven Learner designed by Steven Learner Studio; 123 r Alastair Hendy & John Clinch's apartment in London designed by Alastair Hendy; 124 Anthony Swanson's apartment in London designed by Stickland Coombe Architecture; 125 l Alastair Hendy & John Clinch's apartment in London designed by Alastair Hendy; 125 r Babylon Design Ltd. studio in London; 126 an apartment in London designed by Littman Goddard Hogarth Architects; 127 t Nik Randall, Suzsi Corio, and Louis' home in London designed by Brookes Stacey Randall; 127 b Christian Baquiast's apartment in Paris; 128 t Anthony Swanson's apartment in London designed by Stickland Coombe Architecture; 128 b & 129 bl an apartment in London designed by Littman Goddard Hogarth Architects; 129 tl an apartment in Knokke, Belgium designed by Claire Bataille and Paul ibens; 129 r Chelsea Studio New York City, designed by Marino and Giolito; 130 l Anthony Swanson's apartment in London designed by Stickland Coombe Architecture; 130 c & 131 l Alastair Hendy & John Clinch's apartment in London designed by Alastair Hendy; 130 r Nicki De Metz's flat in London designed by De Metz architects; 131 c Andrew Noble's apartment in London designed by Nico Rensch Architeam; 131 r Lucy Guard's apartment in London designed by Urban Salon; 132–133 Patricia Ijaz's house in London designed by Jonathan Woolf of Woolf Architects; 134 Brian Johnson's apartment in London designed by Johnson Naylor; 135 l Jeff Priess and Rebecca Quaytman's apartment in New York designed by Fernlund and Logan Architects; 135 c Alastair Hendy & John Clinch's apartment in London designed by Alastair Hendy; 135 r Evelyne Roussel's house in Paris; 136 tl Han Feng's apartment in New York designed by Han Feng; 136 b Alastair Hendy & John Clinch's apartment in London designed by Alastair Hendy; 140 Gabriele Sanders' apartment in New York; 144 l an apartment in London designed by Littman Goddard Hogarth Architects; 144 c Alastair Hendy & John Clinch's apartment in London designed by Alastair Hendy; 144 r Brian Johnson's apartment in London designed by Johnson Naylor.

index

acknowledgements

Thank you Andrew Wood, for your great pictures and your appetite for photography, interiors, people, travel, and sushi. Thank you everyone at Ryland Peters & Small, for presenting me with this opportunity. Thank you Anne Ryland, Kate Brunt, Megan Smith, and Annabel Morgan—in the order I first met you—for your commitment and interest in this project; your individual and professional input is evident in the book. Thank you Nadine Bazar, for your essential contribution.

My biggest thanks to everyone living in a single space who said yes to photography and to all the architects and designers whose work is included. Thank you all for your hospitality, inspiration, imagination, and originality. Thank you to everyone who gave me their valuable time and helpful information and suggestions.

Finally, thank you Lawrence Morton. And thank you Atom. Although I long to live in several places in this book, my home is the people I live with.